Guided Reading

One Lesson,
All Levels,
Any Text

Guided Reading

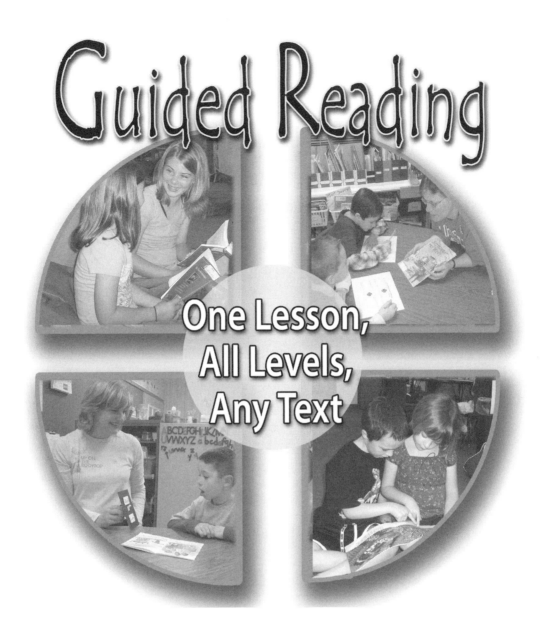

One Lesson,
All Levels,
Any Text

by Tricia Burke and Kathy Hartzold.

Crystal Springs
BOOKS

A division of SDF Staff Development for EDUCATORS.
Peterborough, New Hampshire 03458

Published by Crystal Springs Books
A division of Staff Development for Educators (SDE)
10 Sharon Road, PO Box 500
Peterborough, NH 03458
1-800-321-0401
www.crystalsprings.com
www.sde.com

Published 2007

Printed in the United States of America

11   10   09   08   07   2   3   4   5

ISBN: 978-1-934026-07-6

Library of Congress Cataloging-in-Publication Data

Burke, Tricia (Tricia F.)

  Guided reading : one lesson, all levels, any text / by Tricia Burke and Kathy Hartzold.

     p. cm.

  Includes bibliographical references.

  ISBN-13: 978-1-934026-07-6

  1. Guided reading. I. Hartzold, Kathy. II. Title.

  LB1050.377.B86 2007

  372.41'62--dc22

                    2007019222

Editor: Elaine Ambrose

Art Director, Designer, and Production Coordinator: Soosen Dunholter

Photos: Tricia Burke and Kathy Hartzold

Dedications

This book is lovingly dedicated to my mom for always seeing and appreciating the best in me, my dad (my first and best "turn-and-talk" partner), and my husband, Kevin, and my children, Chris and Emily, for their love and support.

Tricia

To my husband and children for their unending support, patience, and confidence. And to my first and greatest teacher, my mother. Also to Gary Heider, an outstanding principal who believes in and sees the best in his teachers.

Kathy

Acknowledgments

We would like to thank our wonderful editor, Elaine Ambrose. We could not have done this without her!

Dear Teacher,

We know firsthand how time-consuming and overwhelming it is to plan effective reading lessons to meet all of your students' needs. We also know how little time you actually have! We've both been classroom teachers, and now, as reading specialists, we work with many classroom teachers, so we know you want teacher-tested lessons that are easy to follow and that you can use with materials you already have on hand.

We also know you want lessons that lend themselves to differentiation. Our lessons allow you to adjust your reading groups easily and to offer scaffolding to students who need more support.

There are many "right" ways to conduct guided reading instruction. This book is about the lessons themselves. We've designed the core lessons in this book to save you time while helping you provide the quality instruction you demand for all of your students. With these lessons, you'll teach skills that your students will be able to apply across the content areas and throughout the day. Regardless of your knowledge or level of training in teaching reading, you will be able to implement these lessons in your classroom quickly and easily.

We hope this book helps you create lifelong readers and, in the process, brings you joy in teaching reading.

Happy Teaching!
Tricia Burke and Kathy Hartzold

Table of Contents

Chapter 8 Visualizing: Bringing the Story to Life 105

Chapter 9 Inference 114

Recommended Reading & Reproducibles 123

Chapter 1

Guided Reading: What, Why, How

*I*n elementary school, teaching all students how to read is the overwhelming priority. That's not to say math, science, and social studies are unimportant. We teach those, too. But reading takes precedence. To prepare our students for the in-depth content area learning to come, we first must teach them to read. This is an awesome responsibility!

While an elementary class's entire day is infused with literacy, guided reading is the core of a balanced literacy program. It's the time during each day when we are actually teaching our students to become readers. We teach them explicit strategies that successful readers use, and we guide them through the application of these strategies in texts at their instructional levels. Vygotsky's theory of the Zone of Proximal Development explains that the best place for new learning to occur is with text that is not too easy and not too hard, with the guidance of an effective teacher (Vygotsky, 1978). This zone is commonly referred to as a student's instructional reading level. Thus, teaching guided reading has been seen traditionally as forming different groups of students based on similar reading levels and planning individual lessons for each group.

What has made guided reading instruction seem overwhelming for many teachers is the misconception

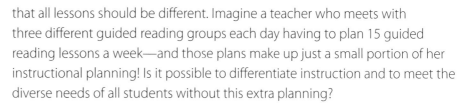

When it comes to guided reading, differentiation can mean using one lesson but with different texts chosen to meet the instructional reading level requirements of each group of students.

that all lessons should be different. Imagine a teacher who meets with three different guided reading groups each day having to plan 15 guided reading lessons a week—and those plans make up just a small portion of her instructional planning! Is it possible to differentiate instruction and to meet the diverse needs of all students without this extra planning?

Differentiation is a buzzword that has been known to cause panic among even the most experienced educators. But it doesn't mean we have a different curriculum for each child or each reading group. Differentiation means making our school's curriculum accessible to all students so that each one experiences success, and guided reading should make learning and applying effective reading strategies accessible to all students.

When it comes to guided reading, differentiation can mean using one lesson but with different texts chosen to meet the instructional reading level requirements of each group of students. In this way, we can teach all learners the same important reading strategies, and they can practice applying each one within their own instructional comfort zone—that place where each child will learn best.

The teacher's roles during guided reading include the following:

- to explain the purpose of the strategy explicitly, including how it will make the students better readers,
- to model how a skilled reader uses the strategy,
- to explain clearly how and when students will use the strategy ,
- to guide learners and scaffold support as they practice the strategy with texts at their instructional levels, and
- to end each lesson by reinforcing the importance and purpose of the strategy and how it will help them be successful readers.

The goal of guided reading is to develop independent readers. As Jane Rambo conveys in the book *Spotlight on Comprehension* (Hoyt, 2004), the purpose of guided reading is not to teach a book so that our students understand that one book, but to teach them reading strategies they can apply to all books. Research demonstrates what good readers do and the strategies they use when they read, and all students need these strategies. Every classroom has learners at various levels of literacy, and the strategies and skills we present in these lessons are critical and accessible for all readers.

Comprehension strategies have been a major focus of recent literature. Regie Routman (*Reading Essentials*, 2002) explains the dangerous message we send students if we focus our reading instruction on simply getting the words right. The purpose of reading is always to understand the text, and even our youngest readers should hear this from us loud and clear and often. Comprehension instruction should be about teaching our students the strategies good readers use to understand text. Good readers question, make connections, determine what is important, visualize, and make inferences as they read (Miller, 2002; Keene and Zimmermann, 1997).

From the very beginning, we must teach students to make meaning from the text they read. Don't wait until they have learned how to read all the words before you turn their attention to thinking about the text and its meaning; even our youngest students need comprehension instruction that focuses on the strategies of effective readers.

So, is it okay to teach the same lesson to all of your groups with different texts? You bet! Think about it this way: if it's okay to teach questioning, for example, to first, second, and third graders, why wouldn't it be okay to teach questioning to your entire class, even though they're at different levels? Not only is it okay to do so, it's smart!

There are many advantages to teaching all of your students the same strategy at the same time. If you've taught them how to determine what's important, for example, and given them practice and support in applying the strategy to texts at their own levels, then you can use that strategy in the content areas. For example, when you teach social studies from their textbook or a social studies weekly, you can refer to what they've learned during guided reading to help them determine what's important and expect them to apply the strategy to their social studies text. You can do this because you know that all your students have received this critical instruction. If you had taught this strategy to just one or two groups, you couldn't remind students to use it during other instructional times of the day.

You'll realize another advantage to this method when you want to move students between groups. Our students progress at different rates, and within guided reading groups there will be students who are ready to move to a different group because their reading has improved and they're ready for more challenging text. There are also times when you want to group students based on similar interests in a nonfiction topic or a particular book. Our plan for teaching guided reading facilitates creating flexible, needs-based groups. By teaching the same strategies and lessons to all, you can move students between groups knowing that they have all had the same instruction. You won't waste valuable time trying to catch students up or worry about instructional gaps or "holes."

Teaching guided reading has traditionally been defined as having groups that rotate between centers and the guided reading table. This can be an effective way to conduct lessons. However, we have found our lessons to be more effective and efficient when we meet with the entire class at once. We do this by teaching the mini-lesson to the whole class. We then distribute appropriately leveled materials to all our students so they can practice applying the strategy they have just learned. This is the "during" portion of the lesson. We scaffold our support by meeting with students as needed. Then we gather as a whole class for the "after" part of the lesson. This method reduces the amount of time and planning our guided reading takes. We no longer have to invent meaningful activities to keep other students engaged while we meet with a group. In a short time, our entire class has received effective, cohesive instruction and has practiced applying the strategy with books at the appropriate instructional levels.

How to Use This Book

Our guided reading lessons have three main parts: before reading, during reading, and after reading. Each component has a specific purpose and function. Each lesson begins with an introduction about the strategy and includes a sample mini-lesson.

Before Reading

If a lesson involves preparation, it is included in this section. More importantly, this is where you will set the purpose for reading. You will explain to students what you want them to do as readers and why it is important, and you will model the strategy for them.

The more explicit your prereading instruction, the more effective your lesson will be. If you are working with groups, you may choose to give a book introduction, based upon the needs of the group and the chosen text, or you may decide to preteach some vocabulary. You'll make these decisions based on your grade level and your students' needs. Think carefully as you make these judgments; the goal is to develop independent readers. You might want to teach your students how to do their own book introductions (see **Get Your Brain Started!** on page 42).

The same is true for vocabulary. Successful readers constantly bump into unfamiliar words, but they're able to use context clues to get close enough to the meaning to keep reading and understanding the text. Our students need these strategies, and we can provide them by explicitly teaching how and when to use each one within the guided reading lessons.

During Reading

Now that you have shown your students what they will be doing, this part of the lesson gives them the opportunity to apply the skill. As they read and practice the strategy you have taught during the mini-lesson, you are individualizing and differentiating your instruction. You can now

work with individual students, scaffolding support as needed. At the same time, you're reinforcing lessons previously taught. For example, if you're reading with a student who is not using word strategies you've taught in earlier lessons, you can remind him about them and scaffold support as he works to master them. Other students may need reminders about fluency while you are encouraging them to use the new strategy. Take this opportunity to individualize and differentiate your instruction.

You will also observe and assess students' reading skills during this part of the lesson. Use this time to read with individual students and to discuss their thinking as they read. Many teachers take running records during this time and eventually have substantial assessments of each student. Observational assessments, or anecdotal records, can be just as valuable as any formal assessments you might administer. Oral reading behaviors such as fluency and decoding skills, along with notes about a student's comprehension and thinking, are recorded and used to make instructional decisions. To make the best use of your observations and assessments, have a system in place that enables you to take notes on each student and find them easily. Be sure to use these informal assessments to guide and plan future instruction as well as to form flexible groups based on instructional needs.

After Reading

Because our goals are to focus on meaning, understanding, and a love of reading, discussion of the text should always take place during this section of the lesson. You'll also want to revisit and reinforce the purpose of the strategy you've taught. To ensure that your lesson is effective, always provide feedback to students about what went well and what still needs work. Discuss how the strategy you taught in the mini-lesson helped them as readers. If you noticed students having difficulty applying the strategy, explain the problem and how they can solve it. If you saw good strategy use, tell them! Your students will always learn from hearing how their peers did something successfully. Again, be explicit; remind students about the purpose of the strategy, why they need to use it, and how it will help them become skillful readers.

	Before Reading	During Reading	After Reading
THE TEACHER	Explicitly models strategy Explains why strategy is important Introduces book and vocabulary if necessary	Scaffolds support of strategy use Assesses individual reading behaviors	Discusses meaning of text Revisits purpose of strategy Encourages discussion of students' strategy use
THE STUDENT	Gets brain started and gives it directions Actively listens and learns purpose for reading	Reads text Applies strategy taught during mini-lesson	Discusses meaning of text Reflects on own success applying strategy Reviews purpose of strategy

Sample Mini-Lesson

This is the lesson in action—teacher talking to students. We have written these so you can "hear" the lesson. These scripts are just suggestions; we've used them, or variations of them, with success. You'll want to tailor these scripts to fit the ages and needs of your students as well as your own teaching style.

Sample mini-lesson

The Role of Guided Reading in a Balanced Literacy Program

While guided reading is the core of literacy instruction, our students need much more to become successful readers and writers. Guided reading is one component of a balanced literacy program. Good literacy instruction must also include shared reading, writing, independent reading, and word study. Each component contributes to the goal of developing students who not only *can* read but also *love* to read.

Shared Reading

Shared reading is another critical part of the literacy day. Its purpose is to encourage reading enjoyment while letting students see how you apply the skills of a successful reader and giving them a chance to try those skills with support. Through shared reading, you interact with students using a shared text in a whole-class setting. It might be a big book, a poem, or multiple copies of a text. By listening, watching, and participating as you lead them through the text, students learn how to be effective readers. Shared reading also lets students practice a skill or strategy before trying it independently.

Writing

Reading and writing go hand in hand. We read to gather meaning and we write to convey meaning. The more students write, the better they understand how to organize their thoughts and use the structure of language to express their ideas. The more they read, the easier it is for them to recognize good writing.

Just as our goal as teachers of reading is to develop independent readers, our goal in writing is to develop capable, skillful, independent writers. We want our students to be able to convey their thoughts, ideas, opinions, and knowledge effectively. And just as we do in guided reading, during writing instruction we show them what good writers do, give them time to practice applying what we've taught, and provide explicit feedback. We begin a lesson by modeling, letting them watch us write and hear our thinking as we make decisions on how best to convey our own thoughts.

During guided reading, we teach students how to read many different types of books and how to read for different purposes. During writing, we teach them how to write for different purposes and different audiences. We want our students to be able to write to persuade, to inform, and to entertain.

Independent Reading

Independent reading time is also important instructional time. You can do individual assessments while students read for enjoyment. You can also learn a lot about a student's strategies and preferences when she's reading at her independent level and you're not guiding her through the text. This is when you see students applying the skills you have taught. Are they monitoring their own reading? Are they actively involved in their texts? Can they apply word-decoding strategies effectively?

There are many ways to organize independent reading time. You might assign each child a day, reading with all of the Monday students, for example, on Mondays. Another way is to make decisions daily about which students you will read with that day. You may need to touch base with some students more often, such as when a student has chosen a book that's a "stretch" for him. Although he may be very motivated, he'll need extra support.

However you organize this time, always begin independent reading by reading aloud and communicating your love of books and joy of reading. After the read-aloud, give students time to read and enjoy books at their independent reading levels.

Word Study

The goal of word study is to increase our students' reading and writing skills. We want them to be able to apply the knowledge of letters, sounds, and words taught during word study to all their reading and writing. Students need authentic opportunities to practice these skills.

Word study includes two important components: phonemic awareness and phonics. Phonemic awareness is an oral process that involves hearing and manipulating sounds; phonics applies the sounds to letters and words. By manipulating or breaking down words into letters, sounds, and patterns orally and in writing, students begin to understand how these letters and sounds come together to form words. During word study, students are actively involved with letters and sounds to create words. The National Reading Panel has reported on the importance of explicitly teaching students to convert letters into sounds and then teaching them to use those sounds to form words. Significant reading gains were reported among kindergarten through sixth-grade readers when teachers employed a systematic approach to phonics instruction (NRP, 2000).

How Does Guided Reading Look? There's No One Right Way

No one right way . . . this really says it all. To find the right format to teach guided reading, you need to consider not only your students but also yourself. What do *you* need as a teacher? Children aren't the only ones who need differentiation—teachers are all different, too, and we all have our own particular needs and strengths. To be the best teachers we can be, we need to take these into account and organize our classrooms accordingly.

Some of us crave structure and order in our classrooms. We just can't function unless we're surrounded by calm, quiet, efficient organization. Other teachers thrive on the buzz of actively engaged students all around them. There's no right or wrong way—whatever you can make work for you and your students is the best way. You have a big job! Give yourself the freedom to do what's most comfortable for you. Find your strengths and use them to organize your classroom and your day in a way that allows you to deliver effective instruction, and your students to receive it.

Children aren't the only ones who need differentiation— teachers are all different, too . . .

Chapter 2

Print Strategies

Word strategies, or decoding strategies, are critical tools for beginning readers. It's crucial to teach our students to think as they read, but before they can really think about what the text means, they have to be able to read the words.

The following strategies are ones that skillful readers use independently and flexibly. While you need to teach each one separately, your students will eventually have to determine for themselves when to use each strategy. This takes practice—as their reading improves, these decisions will become automatic. The *Decoding Strategies* bookmark on page 124 will help students remember to use their strategies as they read.

Shared reading and guided reading provide many opportunities to introduce decoding strategies to students. You can use a big book, chart poem, or overhead transparency to model how and when to use each one. This chapter offers lesson ideas to help you get started.

Decoding Strategies

 Look at the pictures for clues.

 Start the tricky word.

 Think about what would make sense.

 Skip the word and return to fix it.

 Look for chunks you already know within larger words.

 Switch the vowel sound.

Decoding Strategies

While introducing the strategies to students is important, it's only the beginning. The next and most important step is to hold them accountable for using them. It's so tempting to jump in and help when we hear a student stumbling over a word. Step back—bite your tongue if you have to! Students need to realize the job is theirs and these are opportunities to use the tools you've given them. They have to be able to realize when a word doesn't make sense, and then they need to do something about it. They need to decide which strategy to use and when to use it. Once we jump in and tell them what strategy to use, or tell them the word, they become dependent on us to do the work for them.

Look at the pictures for clues.

Illustrations offer information about the story, especially for our youngest readers. Don't cover the pictures. It's a skilled reader who checks the picture for help decoding a tricky word. A picture that shows two cars occupying one space on the road will help a student decode the word "crashed." Always encourage your students to check the pictures.

Start the tricky word.

When a student comes to a word she doesn't know, she should at least start the word with the beginning sound or sounds. This serves two purposes. First, by simply starting the word with the beginning sound or sounds, the correct word may pop into her head. The second benefit of this strategy is that it keeps a student focused on the word. How many times have you seen a student look away from the book as if he were thinking when he comes to a word he doesn't know? This strategy reminds them to stay in the book!

Think about what would make sense.

It is almost impossible to use any strategy without simultaneously using this one. We read to understand. Anything we read needs to make sense to us, and if it doesn't, there's something wrong. Thinking about what would make sense should always be first and foremost in a reader's mind. When your student tries to decode a tricky word, she should always ask herself if her guess makes sense in the text. Likewise, if she misreads a word, she should immediately know the word doesn't make sense, and she should stop and do something about it.

Skip the word and return to fix it.

Sometimes reading past the tricky word to the end of the sentence gives students more clues to help them figure it out. We tell students to start the word, read to the end of the sentence, and then come back to fix the tricky word. When they run into a tricky word, they're starting the word with the beginning sound because we have already taught them to use that strategy. When they read on and then return to fix it, they are thinking about what word would make sense within the text. Most students are successful with this combination strategy.

Look for chunks you already know within larger words.

Instead of seeing words as discrete letters, good readers see words in parts. Word parts, word families, or "chunks" children know can help them decode many words. The /at/ in cat can help them read the words "fat," "chat," and even "attitude." By training students to look for familiar chunks in unfamiliar words, we are giving them an important tool for decoding efficiently.

Switch the vowel sound.

Sometimes a student may have tried the other decoding strategies but is still unable to figure out the word. Switching the vowel sound has been effective with many of our students. While vowels can make many different sounds, they do have two main sounds—long and short. Encouraging students to try switching the vowel sound will help. For example, if your student is reading the word "bread" as "breed," he can switch the vowel sound from long to short to read "bread."

Assessing Your Students' Print Strategies

The best way to assess a student's use of print strategies is through running records. If you haven't had training in giving and analyzing running records, ask your school district to provide it as professional development. Running records are an invaluable tool to help you determine the strengths and confusions of your readers. While the focus of our book isn't running records, there are a couple of tips we can offer.

First, anything a student reads with less than 90 percent accuracy is too hard for her! This means your student should not miss more than 10 out of 100 words. If she does, her comprehension will suffer. Don't believe us? Take an article, block out more than 10 of every 100 words, and ask a colleague to read it. How well did she do? This is also why it's frustrating to hear that a teacher or parent is requiring a child to read something too hard because it's "grade level" material. Without major support, that student will learn very little by muddling through the text, except to hate reading. Be sure your students are reading at their instructional or independent reading levels (90 percent accuracy and above).

Word errors that a child corrects without prompting from you are not counted as missed words. When a student self-corrects, she's using her strategies. Celebrate the success!

Take notes as you listen to each student read. When he comes to a tricky word, what does he do? Does he wait for you to help? Does he try using the print strategies you've taught? Is he fluent? Does he seem to understand what he's reading? Use these notes to drive your instruction and help you determine the student's strategy needs. Also use them to determine whether the book he's reading is at an appropriate level for him.

. . . anything a student reads with less than 90 percent accuracy is too hard for her!

Read the Picture

This is an early lesson for beginning readers. It shows them how illustrations can help readers understand the story and even figure out tricky words. Teachers and parents should never cover up a picture while a child is reading. It isn't "cheating" to look at the pictures—it's good strategy use!

Before reading: Select a big book that has good picture clues for text. Before the lesson, choose several words that might be challenging for your students. Make sure the illustrations provide clues for the words you've chosen. List the words on a chart or on the board and highlight them with highlighting tape in the book.

During reading: Conduct the mini-lesson. Give a brief book introduction and begin reading. When you come to the first highlighted word, read the sentence and stop at the word. Explain to students that you always start the word by saying the beginning sound or sounds. Model this and think out loud as you refer to the picture. Let students hear your thinking as you check to see if the word you think is correct will make sense in the sentence.

Next, ask volunteers to tell you what they saw you doing. They should say that you

- said the first sound of the word,
- looked at the picture,
- thought out loud about what the word could possibly be, and
- tried the word in the sentence to see if it made sense.

For the remaining words, call on volunteers to try the process in front of the class or have students work with partners to figure out each word. Then ask partners to share what they think the words are and how the illustrations helped them.

Sample mini-lesson

" *Isn't it frustrating when you're trying to read and you just can't figure out a word? It happens to all of us! For example, look at these words I have listed. Now, try to figure out what they are in your head.*

" *Wow! That was hard, wasn't it? Luckily, there are many things we can do to help ourselves when we're reading. We call them strategies, and one of the strategies we can use is actually in the picture! Many times the pictures have clues to help with tricky words.*

" *I have chosen this book for us to read today. All the words you just tried to read are in this book. As we are reading, I want you to notice how the pictures help us decode those words!*

After reading: At the end of the lesson, review the purpose of the picture strategy. Remind students that looking at the illustrations in a book is just one thing they can try when they are stuck on a word. It won't always work, but skillful readers know that pictures contain meaning that goes along with the story, and they use that knowledge to help them understand and enjoy what they read.

Student-Created Visuals Enhance Learning

You can spend lots of money on posters for your room—vowel sound posters, color charts, comprehension strategy posters, and more! Often these serve more as wallpaper; students seldom look at them to help them learn. Save money with student-created visuals. When your students create a chart or a poster, they benefit first from the experience of making it. The more important benefit, however, is they'll know what it's for when it goes on the wall and they will be more likely to use it. Students also take pride in seeing their ideas and artwork displayed. These visuals become tools students use to achieve independence as learners. Here are examples of student-generated visuals we like.

- Students use their own names and photos to represent vowel sounds or word chunks. For example, a photo of your student Shane can be used for the /sh/ digraph, or one of Jan can be used for the /an/ chunk.

- A student-made poster showing a box of Band-Aids has the vowel digraphs /ou/ and /ow/. The Band-Aids remind students that these digraphs often say, "OWW!"

- Color-word charts serve two purposes: they remind students how to spell color words, and these words contain useful blends and chunks. Create a color-word chart with your students. Circle the blends, digraphs, or chunks you want them to remember. When children need help reading or writing a word with that chunk in it, refer them to the chart.

- Students can also create thematic word lists with pictures to accompany a unit of study or a season or month of the year. They'll use them for reading and writing.

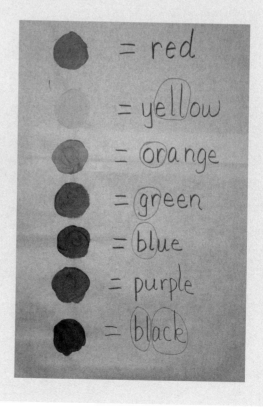

Predicting the Text

This lesson is the opposite of the previous one, but the goal is the same: for beginning readers to see how pictures help tell the story, which makes it easier to read the words.

Before reading: Cover all of the text in the book before you show it to students. Choose a story that relies heavily on illustrations to help young readers.

During reading: Present the mini-lesson. As students offer predictions of some words they might see in the story, ask them to explain what they see in an illustration that makes them think they will see a particular word in the text. Record their word predictions on the board or on chart paper.

After completing a picture walk and recording students' word predictions, uncover the text and read the story to them. Ask them to raise their hands when they hear a word that was predicted and written on the list. Circle the word on the board or chart paper. After reading, discuss the words that were correctly predicted and the words that did not appear in the text.

If you have time, you may want to pass out leveled books and have your students practice applying the picture strategy. Ask your students how the pictures helped tell the story.

After reading: Remind your students that smart readers use pictures to help them understand the story and even to read some of the words.

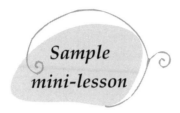

Sample mini-lesson

" *Remember last time we talked about how important illustrations can be when we read? Who can tell me how we use pictures to help us read? Yes, they help us understand the story and they sometimes help us figure out tricky words. Today I have another book for you, but I've covered up all the words! We're going to take a picture walk through the story and really study the illustrations to see if we can tell what's going on and if we can predict some words we might see in the text. I'll write all the words we think we might see, and when we are done with our picture walk, we'll read the story and see how many of our predicted words showed up.*

Mystery Word

This lesson teaches students how strategies can be used together and to always consider meaning when using any strategy.

Before reading: Create sentences with a key word in each one that students can decode using the following strategies: start the mystery word, then read on, and return to think about what word would make sense in the sentence. Write the sentences on index cards, one word per card. Cover the mystery word, except for its beginning sound or sounds, with sticky notes.

During reading: Pass out one word to each student. Have the students line up in the correct sequence, holding their cards up and facing the class. Students will read the sentence to themselves, trying to decode the mystery word using the two strategies. Have them start the word, read past the word, and then return to fix the sentence. Discuss each word your students suggest and whether it makes sense and begins with the same sound. When they've had a chance to do this, ask volunteers to tell you the word. Discuss how they arrived at their guess. Then show them the word. Repeat the process with other sentences, giving word cards to other students in the group until everyone has had a chance to practice using the two strategies together to decode the mystery word.

Remind your students that what they just did with the mystery word sentences is what they should do when they're reading their books today and come to a word they don't know. Then listen to individual students read, scaffold support to students who need it, and praise all of your readers for good strategy use.

After reading: Share some of the successes you observed and discuss how these strategies will make your students better readers.

Sample mini-lesson

" *We have some students holding words that make a sentence. One of them is holding the mystery word. We are going to figure out the mystery word by using two of our strategies at the same time. We will be thinking about what word makes sense and what word starts with the same letter or the same sound. Read this sentence inside your head and try to figure out what the mystery word could be. Use the "what would make sense?" strategy. Remember, you will also be starting the mystery word, so your guesses should make sense and begin with the correct sound. Then we'll uncover the mystery word to see if one of our guesses is correct.*

LESSON FOCUS

Chunking Clues Posters

To help students remember word parts, or chunks, and actually use them, have visuals in your classroom that they have created themselves. Posters on walls make great decorations, but students rarely use them as reading and writing resources. The goal of this lesson is for students to create posters they'll actually use!

Before the lesson: Choose several word chunks you want your students to learn. You can teach this lesson with groups by giving each group a different chunk or it can be a whole-class lesson. Just divide your class into groups and have them create their posters at the same time. Either way, all groups will present their posters so everyone will know what the visuals stand for. Students will need large pieces of oak tag, markers, scissors, and glue sticks. Also have magazines available that they can cut pictures from.

During the lesson: After the mini-lesson, assign each group its word chunk and then visit groups to praise cooperative behavior and creativity, and to offer assistance. You may need to help some groups brainstorm ideas. Make sure each group chooses things that actually represent the sound the chunk makes. For example, we have had students use pictures of their snacks to represent the /ack/ chunk. We are always surprised at how creative our students get when developing their posters!

After the lesson: Each group should present its poster to the class. The groups will explain their visuals and how each one represents their word chunk. Choose a prominent place to display the posters and refer to them often when students are reading and writing. You might also create a class "chunk" book by taking a photo of each group with its poster.

Sample mini-lesson

" *Boys and girls, we have talked a lot about how using parts of words we know, or chunks, can help us read many words. Today we're going to focus on a few important chunks and create posters to help us remember them and how they sound. Then we'll display them in our classroom and use them to help us read and write.*

Here is one I made. Remember how we have been talking about the /at/ chunk? Here's my poster with /at/ written on it. Can you see the pictures on my poster? Who can tell me what they are? Yes—a cat, a bat, and our friend, Matt! Those pictures and words will help us remember what /at/ sounds like. When I see the /at/ chunk in another word I'm trying to read, I can look at this chart and remember that /at/ sounds like the end of cat. Notice that I drew the bat, I cut out a picture of a cat, and I took a photo of Matt. Matt, aren't you lucky to have a name that will help us be better readers!

I'm going to divide you into four groups and assign each group a chunk. Then your group will create a poster to help the whole class when we read and write. Every group has to think of at least three things that remind them of their chunk. You may draw, cut pictures out of magazines, or even find something or someone in the room for me to take a picture of. Be creative!

Student-created visuals become resources that children use to gain independence in their reading and writing.

Teacher Tip

Encourage beginning readers to use the word chunk posters by referring to them often. For example, if you're reading with a group and they get stuck on a word like fling, ask them to point to the poster that has the same chunk.

Challenge Word

This lesson works well with all grade levels. Once your students understand how familiar chunks in words can help them decode a new word, give them plenty of opportunities to practice this strategy. Do this at the beginning of every guided reading lesson. It takes only a minute or two, but the benefits are great. It won't be long before you see students decoding multisyllable words successfully as they read.

Before reading: Choose a multisyllable word and write it on the board or on chart paper. If you use chart paper, you can save the papers for children to refer to later.

During reading: Demonstrate for students how you move from left to right finding and circling chunks you know within the larger word. After circling each one, explain how you knew the chunk. For example, if you were chunking the word "understand," you might circle "un" and write the word "sun" under that chunk, telling students that the word "sun" helps you know how to read the chunk "un." Then continue circling and explaining other chunks. Once all chunks have been circled, put your finger under the beginning of the word and slide it from left to right as you say each part.

Next, write another word and invite a student to be

Here's the word "scientifically" chunked by a third grader.

Scien – it reminds me of science so it will probably be pronounced /scien/.
If – it has the word "if" in it.
Call – I see the word "call."
Y – I know that Amy has a "y" at the end and it's pronounced /ee/.

Sample mini-lesson

" *Boys and girls, now that we know how chunks can help us read bigger words, we're going to practice this every day at the beginning of our reading lesson. Each day you'll see a challenge word on the board. I'll call one of you to come up and show us how to chunk the word to decode it. Let me show you what I mean by chunking this challenge word. Look at this word (gardening). I will start at the beginning of the word and circle "ar." I know the word "car" so I know how "ar" will probably sound. Then, I'll circle "en" because I know how to say Ben; I know how "en" sounds. I'll also circle "ing." The word "ring" from our word wall helps me remember how that will sound. I will put all of the parts together as I track the word. The word is gardening.*

the teacher; he'll begin circling chunks he knows and explaining to the group how he knows each part. It is important to tell your students that even if they know the word, they are not allowed to say it yet. First, they need to take it apart in chunks. If the student is having trouble, he may call on another student to tell him a word part that will help. After the word has been chunked, he puts his finger under the word and slides it from left to right as he says the entire word. This process helps students to write multisyllable words, too.

After reading: Remind students that this activity is good practice for what they should be doing with challenging words they encounter in their reading.

Teacher Tip

- **When you're reading with students, jot down words they have trouble decoding. Use these words the next day with this activity.**

- **Put students' names on Popsicle sticks in a jar and draw one every day to decide who should be the teacher. Then leave that child's stick out until everyone has had a chance to chunk the challenge word.**

- **After a word has been decoded, underline each syllable and remind students that all syllables have at least one vowel. Encourage them to use this information when they write.**

- **Always have students chunk words from left to right, the way they read. Many will try to circle parts of words randomly, which won't carry over to their reading and writing as effectively.**

LESSON FOCUS
Vowel Sound Switch

Switching the vowel sound, which focuses on the short and long sounds of vowels, can be an effective strategy. Because vowels make many sounds, both alone and in combination with other vowels, this strategy should not be overemphasized. Instead, teach it as an option for young readers to try when other strategies haven't helped them decode an unknown word. Show your students plenty of examples of times when this strategy is helpful, as well as times when it is not.

Before reading: Prepare a light switch to use as a visual and a manipulative. You can purchase an inexpensive one at any hardware store. Label the top of the switch "short" and the bottom "long."

During reading: Use the following words for practice, switching the light switch from short to long, and then long to short.

Start with the short vowel sound and switch to the long sound: cone, post, late, gave, chime, dive, deep, these, tune, cute. Then start with the long vowel sound and switch to the short vowel sound: can't, stack, help, next, give, print, lost, pond, must, skunk. Invite your students to think of other words.

As students are reading their books, listen to individuals and notice their strategy use. Make sure they're not overusing

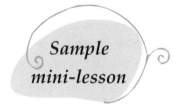

Sample mini-lesson

" *Boys and girls, can you name the letters of the alphabet that are vowels? Yes, that's right—a, e, i, o, and u. Every word in our language contains at least one of these letters. And you know that vowels can make many different sounds, but that they do have two main sounds—the long sound and the short sound. Okay, let's review the long and short sounds of each vowel.*

Now, look at this (hold up the light switch). Who can tell me what this is? You're right; it's a light switch. It turns lights on and off. Well, we're going to use this to help us switch the vowel sound from long to short and short to long! When you're reading and you come to a tricky word, you can try this strategy of switching the vowel sound. This means that if you've tried the short vowel sound but the word does not make sense, you can try switching to the other main sound, the long sound. Let's practice this strategy with some words.

Now that you know how to use this strategy, it's another tool you can put in your reading toolbox. If you come to a tricky word, and you've tried other strategies and still can't read the word, try switching the vowel sound.

the switch-the-vowel strategy, but instead are trying it when other strategies have not worked. When you notice a student using this strategy successfully, make a note of it to share with other students after reading.

After reading: Review the purpose of the strategy and when students should use it. Share successes students had with this strategy while reading.

Use the light-switch manipulative any time you notice a student who needs to review the two main sounds for each vowel.

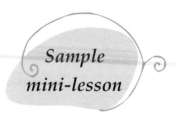

" *Okay, boys and girls, I want you to begin reading this poem and as you read, use your yellow highlighters to highlight any words that are tricky for you.*

Give students a few minutes to read silently and to highlight words they don't know.

" *Next, I want you to reread this poem to yourself. This time, use your reading strategies to figure out those tricky words you highlighted. If you figure out a word you did not know, you will circle that word with your other color highlighter.*

Give students a few minutes to do this; make notes about students' strategy uses and scaffold support to those who need it.

" *Great! You were able to read even more words! Raise your hand if you would like to come up and circle one of the words in the poem that you were able to read because you used your strategies. When you come up, you also need to tell us which strategy helped you solve your tricky word.*

" *Now, let's all read the poem together. We'll read it once slowly and then another time for fluency. After we read it, I'll assign partners, and you can both practice reading it again. Be sure to tell each other what strategies you used to read your tricky words.*

LESSON FOCUS

Word Strategies with Poetry

While this lesson is helpful for any students who need word-strategy practice, it works especially well with first through third graders. You'll also find it effective for reviewing strategies and for encouraging flexibility with strategy use.

Before reading: Each student will need a yellow highlighter and one highlighter of another color. Choose a poem at your students' reading level, and make a transparency of it for the overhead projector or copy it onto large chart paper. In addition, give each student a copy of the poem.

During reading: After conducting the mini-lesson, discuss the poem and its meaning. Encourage students to enjoy the rhythm and rhyme as they read. Have partners read it together, taking turns and switching readers for each new line. Remember, practice makes fluent! Encourage them to use expression to bring the poem's meaning to life. Listen to partners read and make notes about their fluency, comprehension, and use of strategies.

After reading: Briefly review all the strategies you saw students using; praise them for working well together and for becoming strategic readers.

It's Show Time!

Teaching your students word strategies and how to use them is only half the battle. The second half is equally important! Often, students can name all the word strategies you've diligently taught them, and even describe each one in detail. But when they read aloud to us, they don't use them! Hold students accountable for these strategies. Once your students really understand how to use them, don't let them get away with waiting for you to tell them the word or reading on when they have obviously made an error.

Before reading: Make sure each student has a book at his instructional reading level.

During reading: As students are reading, you may want to take running records or simply jot down notes about their strategy use. See page 125, *Individual Strategy Use Assessment,* for a form to use with individual students and page 126, *Class-at-a-Glance Strategy Use Record,* for one you can use to chart the progress of your whole class.

Class-at-a-Glance Strategy Use Record

Name	Date	Looks at the picture	Starts the tricky word	Thinks about what makes sense	Reads on and returns	Looks for chunks	Switches the vowel sound	Notes:

Use these forms to chart the progress of individual students or your whole class as they learn to use decoding strategies.

Individual Strategy Use Assessment

Name _____ Date _____

Title _____ Fiction _____ Nonfiction _____ Level _____

Strategy	Uses Strategy		Comments
Look at the picture for clues.	Yes	No	
Start the tricky word.	Yes	No	
Think about what makes sense.	Yes	No	
Skip the word and return to fix it.	Yes	No	
Look for chunks you already know within larger words.	Yes	No	
Switch the vowel sound.	Yes	No	

Sample mini-lesson

" *Okay readers, today is strategy show day! We have learned all our word strategies and I've really enjoyed watching your reading get better and better as you use these strategies! Today, I'm going to read with each of you and listen to you apply these strategies. Every time I see you trying a strategy, I'll place one M&M in front of you. When we are done, you may eat the candy you earned. So let me see how well you can use your strategies. Remember, when you come to a word you don't know, try a strategy without me reminding you. If I have to remind you, then it doesn't count.*

After reading: When a student finishes reading to you, point out one of the words she did especially well on and praise her strategy use. Remind students that you expect them to use these strategies whenever they read.

Teacher Tip

Use the Class-at-a-Glance Strategy Use Record to help you create flexible needs-based groups for further instruction and practice applying the decoding strategies.

More Lesson Ideas

- **Leave a Clue:** Copy a short passage or poem without illustrations. Make sure your students can read and understand the text first; then explain that they're going to be illustrators and they'll need to put clues in their pictures. Tell them that their illustrations should match the text, so that younger readers can figure out some of the words just by looking at their pictures. Have students choose a few words from the text to leave clues about in their illustrations. For example, if the word "guitar" is in the poem, they'll need to draw a guitar in their illustrations.

- **I Spy:** Choose an illustrated, oversized text. Before the lesson, cut a large magnifying-glass shape from tagboard. Before you read a page, let students help you use the magnifying glass to inspect the illustration for clues. Discuss all the elements of the picture. Now read the page and stop to discuss any words students were able to read because of the picture. Repeat with several more pages. Give young readers their own "magnifying glasses" to do this independently as they read.

Chapter 3

Getting Started

*T*aking time to teach your students the procedures you expect them to follow during guided reading instruction will result in big payoffs for them and for you. If your directions and expectations aren't clear and consistent, you can expect chaos! Before beginning guided reading, determine what those expectations are. Common pitfalls to successful guided reading routines include:

- constant interruptions from students while you are working with others,
- interruptions from students in the group who finish the assigned reading early and don't know what to do, and
- students who blurt out answers.

Teach procedural lessons the same way you teach strategy lessons. First, tell students what you want them to do and why. Then show them what to do by modeling each procedure. Let them practice each one, post your rules where everyone can see them, and refer to them often. The most important step for success comes after you've taught students—hold them accountable for following the rules.

Setting the Procedures for Success

Here is a sample lesson to teach procedures that we have used with success. It works well with the whole class or groups.

Before reading: First, define your procedures and expectations, taking your students' ages and developmental levels into account; decide what's going to work best for you. Make one or two large posters that list your rules and display them where all students can see and refer to them.

During reading: After presenting the mini-lesson, model for students the kinds of behaviors that you don't want to see. Ham it up! They love to see teachers misbehaving. Read a page or two of a book; then stop and loudly announce, "I'm done!" Tap a student and tell her that you're done; ask her what to do. Then stop and discuss how distracting that was for everyone in the group. Next, model reading the pages and then going back and thinking about the story. Let students hear your thinking. Discuss how much better that was for the whole group. Now let your students practice.

Once students have this under control, they're ready for the next step, which is actually easy for them. What's difficult is making yourself follow through! We all teach students to raise their hands to ask or answer questions, but we don't always hold them accountable for doing it. It's so easy to react to a student who answers your question with the exact response you're looking for, but unless he raised his hand, fight the urge! If you respond, you're telling students that in order to be heard they have to talk out. Teach your students the rule and then hold them, and yourself, accountable.

The last procedure is one we've found very useful. While a group is reading, we want to listen to individual students read. Teach them to read silently or "whisper read" unless you tap their hand. If you tap a student, she should begin reading out loud, but softly, from wherever she was on the page. This

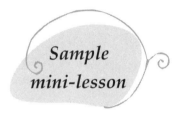

Sample mini-lesson

" *Welcome to guided reading! During this time, we will be working and learning together, and I want you to feel comfortable. I also want you to feel excited—so much learning will take place here! It's exciting for me, too, as I look ahead to the readers you'll become by the end of this year.*

" *To be able to learn all we can, we need to make sure we know how to work together. Whenever we work in a group, we need rules. We will all be responsible for doing our part to make sure this is a place where everyone can learn.*

" *The procedures I am going to teach you are*

- *what to do if you finish an assignment before others in the group finish,*

- *how to get permission to talk or answer questions,*

- *and how to read without disturbing others.*

Many times I will assign pages for you to read. Since everyone reads at different rates, some students will finish before others. Wouldn't it be distracting if you were reading and trying to concentrate and you kept hearing someone say, "I'm done"? Well, it would be distracting for me, too, because I'd have to stop what I'm doing to tell that student what to do next. So our rule during guided reading is that you are never done! If you finish the assignment, you have two choices. You can reread to help you understand the story better, or you can go back and think about the story. Got it? First I'll show you what not to do and then what to do.

lets you move around the table or room quietly to assess and support students. Model this for students and then let them practice. Now you have the procedures in place, and the focus can become teaching reading.

After reading: Take the time to show the students your posters with the rules listed. Read through them once, and then have students read them with you. Remind your students that if they forget what to do, they can always look at the posters. You might want to take photos of students doing a good job following the rules. Display the photos on the posters, changing them every month so that each child is shown successfully following the guided reading procedures.

THE PROCEDURES

1. **What to do if you finish an assignment before others in the group finish:**

   _____

   _____

   _____

2. **How to get permission to talk or answer questions:**

   _____

   _____

   _____

3. **How to read without disturbing others:**

   _____

   _____

   _____

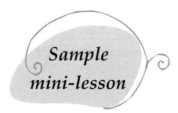

Sample mini-lesson

" *What goes on inside your head when you read? Have you ever tuned into your thoughts as you are reading? Skillful readers have many thoughts. Last night while I was reading, I had so many thoughts! I wondered about so many things that I had to stop and think about what the author was saying. That makes reading exciting!*

" *Today I want you to focus on your thoughts as you read. What are you thinking? I'm going to give each of you two sticky notes. As you read, notice what you're thinking about and write two of your thoughts on the sticky notes. Leave them on the edge of the page where the thoughts occurred; we'll share our thoughts at the end of the lesson.*

LESSON FOCUS

What Are They Thinking?

Before you begin to teach comprehension strategies, it's important to know what your students are already thinking as they read. Many are probably involved with the text and doing a lot of good thinking about the characters, the plot, and so on, but others may not be involved with the text at all. The goal of this lesson is to learn about your students and what they need from you. You can use this lesson to organize your guided reading groups by comprehension needs, or you may want to have students who read at different levels in each group so that those with weaker skills have opportunities to hear good discussions about text.

Before reading: Choose a fiction text at the appropriate reading level for students. Have enough sticky notes handy that you can give each student two or more, depending on grade and ability level. Give a brief book introduction and assign the pages to be read.

During reading: As students read, observe some of the thoughts they're writing. Provide support as needed. Take notes on individual students; you should get a pretty good picture of which ones are at a literal comprehension level, which readers know how to be involved with text, and which students don't "hear" their thinking as they read at all.

After reading: When most students have finished, gather their attention. Ask students if they were surprised at how many thoughts they had while they were reading. Explain that the words in a book don't tell the story by themselves. To really read and understand, the reader has to make the story come to life by thinking about and reacting to the text. Next, invite students to share one of their thoughts and share one of your own. Before students leave the guided reading group, challenge them to continue to tune into their thoughts whenever they are reading. If you wish, students can write their names on their sticky notes and you can collect them to use for planning lessons or creating groups.

To really understand text, readers need to think about and react to what they are reading.

Thinking About Nonfiction

Reading nonfiction is challenging for young readers. The topic may change from page to page, and the text may include unfamiliar vocabulary. Students need to be taught how to be smart and purposeful nonfiction readers. Just as with fiction, it's important to know what your students do when they encounter nonfiction text. What strategies, if any, do they use? What are they thinking? How do they go about engaging with the text? Again, this lesson will teach you more than it will teach your students. Use it to learn how familiar your students are with nonfiction, and whether they have strategies in place to read nonfiction successfully.

Before reading: Explain to students that just as with fiction, our brains need to be actively involved with nonfiction text. During this lesson, you'll want to do a lot of observing. Instead of giving students a book introduction, simply hand the books out and watch what they do. You'll learn a lot by seeing how they begin to read a nonfiction text.

During reading: After you give students their books, really watch them! Take notes about which students just open to page one and begin reading from the top of the page to the bottom. Notice students who spend a few minutes looking through the book, reading the headings, looking at pictures or maps, and so forth. These are often the students who will have less trouble comprehending nonfiction text. Students with little understanding of what they're reading have thoughts focused on individual words. They may be thinking, for example, "What does omnivore mean?" rather than focusing on the broader meaning. Most nonfiction texts will give contextual clues, definitions, and graphics to explain specific terms; not all readers know that.

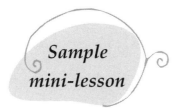

Sample mini-lesson

" *Today you will be reading from page _____ to page _____. Just as we have done before, I want to know what thoughts you have as you read. What are you thinking? What are you wondering? Record two of your thoughts on sticky notes and leave them on the pages where the thoughts occurred. After we finish reading, we'll share some of our thoughts and what caused us to have them. Here is your book; you can get started!*

Skillful readers know that nonfiction texts often give contextual clues, definitions, and graphics that readers need to pay attention to.

After reading: Ask students to share their thinking, having them refer to the text. Ask them to read the part that caused them to have a particular thought. This accomplishes two things. First, you're holding them accountable for having text-connected thoughts—they can't just make something up or state a fact they already know about the topic. Second, this lets all students hear the process of thinking. For example, a student reading about frogs says that one of his thoughts was that frogs would be harder to catch than toads. That can be a good thought, but it's much more effective if the student tells you that the reason he had that thought was because the book said frogs are faster than toads and spend most of their lives in water. This kind of response shows that this student is really thinking—he's connecting what he reads to his own thoughts and inferring something new! Allowing other students to hear this kind of thinking gives them insight to the whole process of thinking while reading. This doesn't always come naturally for our struggling readers.

Get Your Brain Started!

The purpose of guided reading instruction is to create independent readers, so it's important to teach students what to do before they start a new book. Watch your less able readers. You will notice that many of them just take the book, open to page one, and start reading.

Good readers, on the other hand, know what to do! Think about your own reading. The next time you get a new book, pay attention to what you do before you start reading. Chances are you read the title and start thinking. You probably read the back cover and think some more. Maybe you check to see if there is a list of other titles by this author. You might look for a "bio" to see where she's from. All this time you're thinking, but you haven't begun to read. You flip through the book and think. Finally, you're ready to focus on the book—good readers *think* first! Their brains are fully engaged before they've even started to read.

Before reading: Choose books at the instructional level of your students. Make copies of the bookmark *Get Your Brain Started* on page 127. Depending on your grade level, you might also want to use the bookmark *What Did You Think?* (page 128). You can create a double-sided bookmark with these two reproducibles or use the second one in a separate lesson.

During reading: Show students a book you will read and model reading the title and wondering aloud what the story might be about. Notice and talk about any illustrations on the front and back covers. Model checking the back of the book to see if there's a "blurb" or summary. Look through the

Get Your Brain Started And Give It Directions!

How?

Read the title and **THINK!**

Read the back and **THINK!**

Look through the book and **THINK!**

Now your brain is ready to read!

Sample mini-lesson

" Boys and girls, today I'm going to teach you something I want you to do whenever you pick up a book to read. Don't just turn to the first page and start reading. Your brain won't be ready! You have to start your brain and give it directions. Think about it this way. If you go home today *and your mom says, "Hey, let's go to Dairy Queen!" and you both jump in the car and just sit there, will you get to Dairy Queen? Of course not! Your mom has to start the car and give it directions. She has to make the car go where she wants it to go.*

" *Your brain is the same way! If you don't start your brain and give it directions before you begin to read, it will be very hard to focus and understand what you are reading. Today I'm going to show you what good readers do to get their brains started and give them directions. Your job will be to pay close attention and be ready to share what you noticed me doing to start my brain.*

" *Okay, who can tell me what I just did? Yes, I read the title and wondered what the story might be about. You're right! I read the back cover and thought some more. I looked through the book for illustrations, and I thought some more! Do you notice that I keep referring to thinking? That's because it's the most important thing to do to give our brains directions. Now it's your turn to practice what good readers do. I am going to give you the book we'll be reading and we're going to get our brains started and give them directions!*

book quickly and think aloud about the story, verbalizing your predictions about the setting, the characters, and the plot.

Pass out the books and refer students to the title. Let them share what their brains are thinking. Do the same thing with the back of the book, if appropriate, and then ask them to look through the book and again share what they are thinking. Older students reading chapter books can read the chapter titles, if included, and share their thoughts. Discuss how much they already know before they've even started to read, and how focused their brains are. Hand out the bookmark Get Your Brain Started and read it with your students. Have them use it with books during independent reading, too.

After reading: Review the purpose of starting our brains and giving them directions before we read. Remind students that they should do this every time they start reading, not just when they are reading with you.

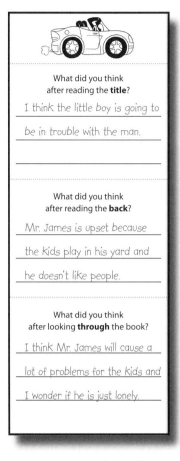

What did you think
after reading the **title**?

I think the little boy is going to
be in trouble with the man.

What did you think
after reading the **back**?

Mr. James is upset because
the kids play in his yard and
he doesn't like people.

What did you think
after looking **through** the book?

I think Mr. James will cause a
lot of problems for the kids and
I wonder if he is just lonely.

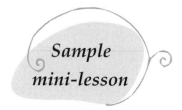

Sample mini-lesson

" *Have you ever played on a sports team? Did you start out knowing how to play the game perfectly? I bet you needed coaching. If you were playing basketball, and your team was down by one point and you had the ball, would your coach run out, grab the ball, and make a basket for you? Why not? Well, your coach's job is to help you learn to be the best player you can be and how to make that shot yourself, not do it for you!*

" *This year, each of you will be a coach—a reading-partner coach! Many times during the year I will ask you to work with a partner during reading. Some days, I may have you take turns reading aloud with your partner; other times, I may have you work together to find answers to questions about the book you are reading.*

How to Be a Reading-Partner Coach

Many of the lesson plans in this book require students to work with partners. To do this well, students must be taught specific procedures. They have to know what's expected of them before they can deliver. After you have modeled this, you'll want to give them plenty of practice, and then hold them accountable.

There are no hard and fast rules for assigning partners; it has worked best for us to pair students at similar reading levels. With younger students, we have found it helpful to keep partners together for quite a while; they develop a routine and a relationship. Also, younger students often have a harder time changing routines. They gain confidence by working with the same partner.

Our older students, on the other hand, enjoy changing partners often. In fact, they benefit from the experience of working with different students. Their conversations about books are more in-depth in these grades, and it's good for them to hear other students' ideas and points of view.

Before reading: First, determine what expectations you will have of reading partners as coaches. Make a short list of your rules and expectations and post them where all students can easily see and refer to them.

During reading: After you've introduced the rules, model how a good reading-partner coach does his job. Have a student read a couple of pages to you. Whenever he struggles, encourage him by suggesting decoding strategies he can try.

Being a partner is like being a coach. You and your partner will help each other be the best readers you can be. For example, if your partner is reading aloud to you and she's having trouble with a word, will you just tell her the word? No! That really wouldn't help her. Just like the basketball coach, your job is to help your partner learn what to do to help herself. If you tell her the word, she still won't know what to do the next time she comes to a tricky word. Your partner will do the same for you.

Good coaches do other things, too. They really listen when their partner is reading or talking, and they're always supportive and kind. Here's a poster of the basic coaching rules. Let's read and discuss each one.

1. *Help your partner figure out how to do it. Don't do it for him or for her!*

2. *Be a good listener.*

3. *Be kind and supportive—treat your partner the way you want to be treated.*

If everyone follows these rules, we'll all learn more and be smarter readers. Who would like to be my reading-partner coach and help me model what a good partnership looks and sounds like? As we are modeling this, keep our three rules in mind. Watch us carefully and be ready to discuss how well we followed them.

Switch roles and let the student be your coach. Discuss the modeling and how the three rules were demonstrated. Early in the year, review the rules often, especially before you assign partners for a particular lesson.

Next, assign reading-partner coaches and let your students practice the rules by taking turns reading aloud. One student reads a page while the other coaches and then they switch roles. We always teach students to read shoulder to shoulder, with all eyes on the book. This way, the focus remains on the book and there is less chance for their attention to wander.

After reading: Gather the group back together and discuss their coaching experiences. Ask them whether they felt they were able to follow all three rules. Each time a lesson requires working in partners, remind students of the three partnership rules, and then hold them accountable for following them.

Sample mini-lesson

> " *Boys and girls, today we are going to talk about something that makes each of you unique. It is called schema, and it's like a fingerprint. Just as no one has the exact same fingerprints as you, no one has the exact same schema.*

> " *Schema is everything you already know and everything you have experienced since you were born. All of this information is stored in your brain, and it affects how you relate to the world and even how you relate to books. When you are reading a story, your schema may tell you, "Hey! I already know a little about this!" Your schema can help you understand the story better.*

> " *Think about what is in your schema. Each of you will make a poster of some of the things in your schema. When we're done, we will see how different we all are, and how alike we are in some ways. First, I'll show you my schema poster.*

LESSON FOCUS

What's in Your Schema?

Schema refers to all the information that we already know and bring to any text. It is what allows us to relate to other ideas and experiences. We use schema to make connections. Students come into our classrooms with different schemas. In this lesson, you will get a glimpse of each child's schema. This will help you guide your students toward the right book selections.

Before the activity: You will need an overhead projector, black paper, a white crayon, and old magazines or printouts of clip art. Read through the mini-lesson and create your own schema before the lesson. Students need scissors and glue sticks.

During the activity: Trace each child's profile using the overhead and black paper. As you are tracing, discuss what he's thinking of putting in his schema.

" Here is a visual of my schema. I know about basset hounds because I have one. I also know about Hawaii, teaching, and Illinois. I've had many experiences and I've been lots of places, so I've included some of these in my schema.

" Now it's your turn. I will trace your profile on black paper, and while you're waiting for me to do that, you can look through these magazines and clip art for pictures of things in your schema. Think about all the things you know or have experience with. Do you have pets? Do you play sports? Are you a brother or a sister? When you find something that's in your schema, cut it out. You may draw what you want to put into your schema, too. When I've done your profile, glue your pictures onto your profile where your brain would be. I think you'll be surprised when you realize how much you already know and all of the information you have in your schema! Remember, these are things you've had experience doing or things you know about.

After the activity: Have volunteers share their schema profiles. Discuss the differences and similarities you see. Ask them what kinds of stories they may be able to relate to because of what's in their schema. Post their schema profiles on the wall so that when they are looking for a book to read, they can recall what's in their schema and choose something they are familiar with and interested in.

Creating schema profiles helps young readers to become aware of what they already know and to bring that knowledge to their reading.

Activate Prior Knowledge for Nonfiction

Activating students' prior knowledge before they read is important. Make sure your students understand what prior knowledge means and how using it helps them comprehend what they read. Even the slightest knowledge about a topic helps students become more involved when reading.

Before reading: Have nonfiction texts at your students' instructional levels. They will also need six to eight sticky notes per pair. Remind your students about their schemas and how they bring their own unique background of experience to their reading. This lesson can be used with any nonfiction topic. This example uses a book about sharks. Before they read, pairs of students will work together to list everything they already know about these fish.

During reading: Remind students that they already know a lot about sharks, and then have them read to confirm that information and to locate new information. Tell them also to watch for misconceptions they may have had prior to reading. Give each pair six to eight sticky notes and ask them to record any facts they find especially interesting. Remind them that photos, graphs, charts, maps, diagrams, and other graphics in nonfiction texts are great places to start.

After reading: When you call them back together, have each pair share their list. Compile all their information on chart paper and praise them for doing a good job. Ask them how activating their prior knowledge about sharks helped them to understand as they read. Did they discover whether anything on the list was incorrect?

Sample mini-lesson

" *Today we are going to learn how activating our prior knowledge, or what we already know about a subject, can help us better understand what we read. Look at this book and tell me what you think we'll be learning about when we read it.*

" *That's right, we'll learn about sharks. There has been a lot of news lately about sharks. Let's see if we can learn more about them and why they behave as they do. Before we start reading, I want to know how much you already know about sharks. You are going to work with your partner to write everything you both already know about sharks. I'll give you five minutes, and then we'll share our information.*

" *Now, we'll use all that we already know about sharks to help us understand what we will read. Our brains are focused and ready to learn. Let's see what new information we can add to our prior knowledge.*

Metacognition: Keep Your Car on the Road!

Teaching students to be aware of their own thinking is one of the hardest things to do. It's also one of the most important tools we can give them to help them become lifelong learners. How often have you read with a student only to have her tell you that she has no idea what she read? Isn't that one of the most frustrating moments as a teacher? We need to teach our students to know when they know and understand what they are reading, and more importantly, to recognize when they **don't** know or understand what they're reading.

Before reading: Choose books for students at their instructional level.

During reading: Conduct the mini-lesson. Pass out books and instruct students to begin reading. Tell them to really focus on their thinking as they read, and if their brains go off the road, they should stop and make their brain go the way they need it to go.

After reading: Ask students if they heard their brain talking about the story while they were reading. Ask if they heard it talking about other things. Praise them for tuning into their thoughts and remind them that being aware of going "off the road" is the first step. Remind them, too, that they're in control and can give their brain directions and keep it on the road.

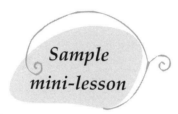

Sample mini-lesson

" *I'm going to ask a question, and I want you to be honest. If you went home after school today, and your mom said it was time to read for half an hour, how many of you would say to yourself, "Yes! I get to read"? Be honest! How many would say, "I don't want to read"? Let me tell you if you haven't yet discovered your true love of reading, it's because you just haven't found the right book—yet!*

" *If I could make one wish, it would be that this year you find the book that does it for you! There's nothing like reading a book that "catches" you and makes you want to read more. I'm still finding books like that. I have one at home right now, and if the principal told me I could do anything I wanted today, I'd rush home and read it. I can't wait to find out what happens next!*

Finding the book that does it for you takes some work. I'm going to write a long word on the board. Don't say it; just look at the word.

Write "metacognition" on the board.

Did you know there are scientists who study how our brains learn? And because of them, I know what your brain is doing right now. It's looking for chunks of that word it knows and seeing parts that remind it of other words. Who can tell me a chunk of this word that reminds you of other words you know?

Possible responses include met, cog, like dog or log, -tion like in action, subtraction, and vacation. Circle word parts as students respond.

Now that you know all these chunks, let's put them together: met-a-cog-ni-tion. Put them together quickly: metacognition. This big word just means you know when you know something, but you also know when you don't know, and you do something to fix it.

Let me explain it this way. We talked about starting your brain and giving it directions before you read. We compared our brains to a car that has to be started and given directions before you can drive anywhere, right? Well, think of your brain as a car again. Not only do you have to start it and give it directions—you have to keep it on the right road! You don't want to go off the road or take a wrong turn. You have to control your brain and make it go where you want it to go.

Maybe your brain is taking a wrong turn right now. You look like you're listening; you're looking at me, but maybe you're really thinking about recess or lunch. You're in charge of your brain. Get it back on the right road! When you're reading, you have to make your brain go where you want it to go.

The first step is to train yourself to know when your brain has stopped understanding or paying attention. Then, you need to figure out what to do when you realize you've made a wrong turn. Today we'll work on the first step. Your brain is always talking to you. Not only will you hear your brain say the words you're reading, you'll also hear it talking to you about the story. If your brain stops talking about the story and starts talking about other things, like what's for lunch, you're not reading effectively! This happens to readers all the time. The difference between a good reader and one who struggles is that a good reader knows when it happens and does something about it!

When you find the book that does it for you, tell me the title so I can share it with others who are still searching for the right book. Next time, we'll talk about what to do when your brain does go off the road.

How to Get Back on the Road

After your students have learned about metacognition and practiced "thinking about their thinking" and whether their brains are on the right road, teach them the next step: what to do when their brains go off the road. How do they get back into the book?

Before reading: Prepare an overhead transparency of the bookmark *Use Your Metacognition* on page 129 for use with the whole class or make a large poster-board version. Make copies of the bookmark for each student.

During reading: Conduct the mini-lesson. As your students are reading, observe partners working through the process and scaffold support as needed. You might ask older students to record the answers to the first part of the bookmark on the back if they have time.

Sample mini-lesson

" *Have you been tuning into your thinking since our last lesson? How many of you have caught your brains making wrong turns or going off the road? Were they thinking about something else? It happens to all of us. Now that we know how important it is to catch our brains when they stop paying attention, let's learn how to fix the problem.*

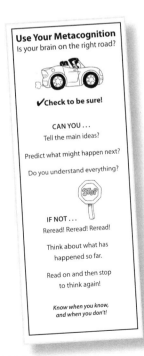

Use Your Metacognition
Is your brain on the right road?

✔Check to be sure!

CAN YOU . . .
Tell the main ideas?

Predict what might happen next?

Do you understand everything?

STOP

IF NOT . . .
Reread! Reread! Reread!

Think about what has happened so far.

Read on and then stop to think again!

Know when you know, and when you don't!

When our brains take a detour, we can't just tune back in and keep on reading. We missed everything that happened while we were on the wrong road! We have to go back and find the spot where we lost our way. I have a special bookmark for you that will help you get into the habit of making sure you are tuned into the book.

Hand out copies of the bookmark Use Your Metacognition.

I will assign reading-partner coaches, and you'll help each other tune into your thinking. You and your partner will read two pages. First, one of you will read while the other follows along. Then you'll stop and your partner will coach you through the bookmark.

The first part of the bookmark asks you to tell the main idea and predict what might happen next, and then asks if you understood what you read. If you can't tell your partner the main idea or predict what might happen, or if you don't feel like you really understood what you read, you'll need to use the strategies under the stop sign to fix your comprehension. You can choose to reread, stop and think about the story and what has happened so far, or read a little bit farther, stop, and see if you're back in the story and understand what's going on. Remember— really pay attention to your thinking. If your thinking about the story stops, you are probably off the road. Do something fast!

After reading: Bring your group back together and discuss how they used their metacognition. Did they notice when their brains took a wrong turn? What did they do to get back into the book? Share some of the successes and challenges you observed. Remind them that with practice this process will become automatic.

Don't Stop the Movie!

Here's another way to teach metacognition. For students to be successful readers, they have to take control of their thinking. If they don't notice when their understanding breaks down, they won't be able to fix it. The easiest way to explain this to students is to use an analogy they can understand, and what child doesn't understand movies?

Before reading: Make an overhead transparency or large tagboard model of the bookmark *How's the Movie?* on page 130. Make a copy for each student as well. Choose a short book or chapter that you can read aloud to model the strategy. Also, choose books at your students' instructional levels that they can read to practice applying the strategy.

Sample mini-lesson

" *What's the last movie you watched? Did you watch it all? If I ask you to tell me about it, can you still see it in your head? What happens if your mom makes you turn off the movie halfway through? Can you still see the whole movie? Of course not!*

" *Well, reading is the same way. When you're reading and understanding, it's like a movie in your head! You can see the story. But when your brain stops understanding, the movie stops. Skillful readers recognize when the movie in their heads stops. If you were watching a DVD, and I pushed the off button on the DVD player, would you watch the whole DVD again? No! You'd try to find where you left off, wouldn't you? The same thing is true with reading.*

How's the Movie?
Do you see it?

✔ **Check to be sure!**

ASK YOURSELF:

Do you see it?
Does it make sense?

IF NOT . . .

Reread! Reread! Reread!
Go back and think!

If you can see the movie,
I hope you enjoy the
rest of the book!

*Know when you know,
and when you don't!*

If you discover that your brain has tuned out of the story, or you don't understand what you read, you have to "rewind the book" to the last place you "watched." Find the last place you understood the text. This takes practice! The hardest part is knowing when the movie in your head stops.

Introduce the bookmark to your students.

I call this bookmark How's the Movie? It will help you tune into your thinking as you read. I also have a book for you. I'll place this bookmark halfway through my book. I'll read and stop when I get to it. Then I'll replay the movie in my head by telling you what the story was about. Your job will be to help me decide whether my movie stopped while I was reading, or if I got it all. If my movie stopped, you'll need to help me figure out where that happened so I know where to start to reread.

Read to students, and when you get to the bookmark, stop and retell only part of what you read. Have students help you go back to find the last place you can remember "seeing the movie."

Thanks for helping me. Do you see how stopping to think really helped? What would have happened if I had just kept reading? You're right; I would have missed most of the story. Now, you're going to do the same thing while you're reading. Place your bookmark on page____. When you get there, stop and use the bookmark to help you replay the book. If you can't replay what you have read, you'll need to find the place where your movie stopped and reread. I will be coming around to listen to some of your movies.

During reading: Give each student a bookmark and let them start reading. Work with individual students; listen to their retellings to learn whether they are noticing when their comprehension breaks down. Use your observations and notes to help you determine which students need more support and practice to master this strategy.

After reading: Gather your group back together. Discuss how keeping the movie in their heads playing while they read helped them understand the story. How did stopping to make sure they were on track help? Did any of them need to stop and reread? Share successes and challenges.

Turn and Talk

Discussion is crucial to the development of higher-level comprehension skills, so we teach our students a procedure called Turn and Talk. The goal is to be able to pose a discussion question and have students immediately turn to their partners and begin a discussion.

The poster on page 131 lists three simple rules. You might want to adapt them for your grade or your students' developmental levels. Explain the rules and model an inappropriate turn-and-talk session with a student volunteer. Your class will gladly tell you what you did wrong. Then model a successful turn and talk that follows your rules.

Turn and Talk

1. **Make eye contact.**
2. **Be respectful.**
3. **Stay on task.**

It's important to point out and model the difference between talking and telling. Telling sounds like this: "What was your favorite part of the book? Mine was . . ." On the other hand, talking involves listening to your partner, taking an interest in what she says, and then offering feedback or asking a question to further the discussion.

An analogy children can understand is a game of ping-pong. The discussion should move back and forth between them like a ping-pong ball. This is hard for some students at first, but if your expectations are clear, and you hold them accountable, even your youngest students can engage in amazing discussions.

When students are starting to turn and talk, keep discussion times brief. It's better to end the session early before they get bored and go off task. With practice, the length of time they are able to sustain good discussions will increase. Explain to your students that sometimes they will not finish discussing a question before you call their attention back to you, but when you do, they immediately become your partner. They should be facing you and making eye contact with you.

With practice and clear guidelines, even young readers can engage in amazing discussions.

Chapter 4

Fluency

*I*n recent years, fluency has emerged as an important factor in successful reading instruction. Slow, choppy reading makes comprehension difficult. Thus, teachers have searched for various effective strategies to help their students develop fluency. To design effective lessons, we first must understand what fluency means. The term actually encompasses three major components:

1. Rate – the speed of reading

2. Accuracy – reading text correctly

3. Prosody – expression and phrasing

Rate: Our brains are designed to process information in chunks. Try having someone talk to you, pausing after each word. It's almost impossible to keep up with what is being said. Students who read very slowly almost always have comprehension problems. Recommendations for how many words per minute a student should be able to read at each grade level can be found in many reading texts and at reading Web sites. You can use these guidelines to do a quick assessment of your students' reading rates.

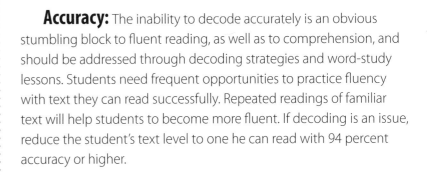

Fluent reading brings a story to life and allows the meaning to come through. It is so much more than error free, fast reading!

Accuracy: The inability to decode accurately is an obvious stumbling block to fluent reading, as well as to comprehension, and should be addressed through decoding strategies and word-study lessons. Students need frequent opportunities to practice fluency with text they can read successfully. Repeated readings of familiar text will help students to become more fluent. If decoding is an issue, reduce the student's text level to one he can read with 94 percent accuracy or higher.

Prosody: Fluent readers make a story come to life with phrasing and expression, or prosody. Without the first two components of fluency, this third component is impossible. A student reading with expression and meaningful phrasing is more likely to comprehend the material, and that, of course, is the goal.

The lessons in this chapter are designed to show students what fluent reading is and to teach each component explicitly. We have purposely placed this chapter before the comprehension chapters because fluency alone can sometimes clear up comprehension problems that students experience.

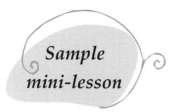

Sample mini-lesson

LESSON FOCUS
Charting Punctuation

Fluency and its relationship to comprehension has been the subject of much current research indicating a positive correlation between the two. As teachers, we tend to go along with what the research shows. Many schools and districts have begun giving timed fluency tests to measure the correct number of words per minute, and timed tests do have their place.

However, fluency is not just about speed; it's also being able to take text and turn it into expressive, meaningful phrases that convey the author's intent. Working with struggling readers, we became aware that often they overlooked punctuation. Students didn't know how to use it to gain meaning. This lesson, ideal for the whole class as well as small groups, teaches students what to do when they come to the most basic punctuation marks.

Before reading: Create a large poster and a transparency of the punctuation chart on page 132. Display the poster where students can see it and you can refer to it as you

Teach students how to "read" punctuation.

> " *We have talked about how an author does everything she can to help us understand her story. The author gives us the words and sometimes uses illustrations. Authors also use something else. Look at the first page of your book and tell me what else you see. Yes, writers use punctuation! Punctuation tells us what to do with our voice and gives us insight into a character's thoughts and feelings. If you don't pay attention to punctuation, understanding*

*the author's words becomes almost impossible!
Just as you have to read the words in a book, you
also have to read the punctuation. Let's try an
experiment. I am going to pass out this page I
have typed from your book. You'll see that all the
punctuation is missing. Try reading it!*

" *Did you notice how much harder your brain
had to work to make sense of what you were
reading? Did you notice how much longer it took
to read? Today we are going to learn how to
use a punctuation chart to remind us what our
voices need to do when we see punctuation.*

read with students. You may want to make a smaller version for each student as well. You'll also need to choose a page from a book your students are working on. This can be your current read-aloud if you wish. Type up the page, but leave out all marks of punctuation.

```
┌─────────────────────────────────────────┐
│            Punctuation                  │
│                                         │
│  When we see _____, our voice _____. │
│                                         │
│      .    =    Drops and stops          │
│                                         │
│      !    =    Gets excited and stops   │
│                                         │
│      ?    =    Goes up and stops        │
│                                         │
│      ,    =    Takes a short rest       │
│                                         │
│    " "    =    Gets to be an actor      │
│                                         │
└─────────────────────────────────────────┘
```

During reading: Use the punctuation chart to guide your discussion. We found it worked best to label the chart: When we see_____, our voice _____. This tells students exactly how to apply the rules to their own reading. Now you can give students the same passage with punctuation included. Tell them to apply the rules from the chart to read the passage fluently and effectively.

After reading: After all students have read the passage, discuss how the punctuation helped their reading. Next, ask volunteers to read sentences from the passage aloud using the punctuation chart rules. Remind students to apply these punctuation rules anytime they are reading.

Meaningful Phrasing

It's hard to listen to a student with awkward phrasing read. Maybe she isn't reading word by word anymore and is stringing a few words together in phrases, but it still doesn't sound right. Meaningful phrasing comes naturally to good readers, but our beginning and struggling readers may need explicit instruction about what meaningful phrasing is, and how it relates to understanding. The easiest way to teach meaningful phrasing in reading is to begin with spoken language.

Before reading: Choose books appropriate for your students' instructional levels.

During reading: After you have presented the mini-lesson, listen to individual students read and provide support as needed. To guide your instruction, make notes about students who struggle with phrasing. Scaffold support to these students at independent reading time or during this portion of any guided reading lesson.

After reading: Gather students back together. Ask volunteers to read one or two sentences of their choice with fluency. Praise your students for tuning into phrasing and remind them that when they don't understand what they have read, they should try rereading with different phrasing. Many times this will fix comprehension problems.

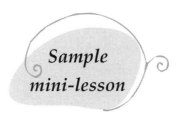

Sample mini-lesson

" *Guess what?* (Say the next sentence slowly; stop after every few words.)

" *Last night I . . . took my daughter to . . . the grocery . . . store. What do you think about how that sounds? What did I say? Was it hard to understand me? What was I doing wrong? You're right! I was chopping my sentence up, almost into separate words. It didn't sound natural, did it? Watch as I write it the way I said it. I'll make a dash wherever I paused. Who wants to say it the way you think I should have?*

As a student repeats your sentence, rewrite it with her phrasing. It should look like this: Last night – I took my daughter – to the grocery store.

Discuss how it now makes sense.

Can you hear how much better that sounds? Some words just make sense to say together. If you spoke a different language and didn't understand English, it would be very difficult for you to tell where one word ends and another begins because we string our words together in meaningful phrases. For example, it just makes sense to say "last" and "night" together. We do this naturally when we talk, and good readers do it when they read.

Let's practice! Someone asked me what I had for dinner last night. Here's what I said. (Write this on the board or overhead.)

I had spaghetti and meatballs and mom made a salad. Of course, she made my favorite garlic bread to go with it!

ways. Discuss how the meaning is clearer when we read with natural phrasing.

Now, think about reading. When we read fluently, our phrases are just as natural as when we're speaking. If we read in awkward phrases, we lose meaning; it's harder to understand the author's words. Pay careful attention to your phrasing as you read today.

Look at the first paragraph in your book. Read it in your head first, and then we will talk about the phrasing you used.

Have volunteers read one or two sentences aloud and invite students to discuss their phrasing. Did they sound natural? Were they easy to understand?

Now you're ready to read the rest of your book fluently, with meaningful phrasing.

Read this silently and think about the phrasing you use. Where does it make sense to string words together? Where does it make sense to pause?

Discuss appropriate phrasing in these sentences. Invite several students to try reading the sentences a couple of different

Sample mini-lesson

" *Remember this book we read? Help me retell the story.*

" *We have talked about how an author uses punctuation to help you know how he wants you to read his words, and we created a chart to remind us what our voices should do when we see the different punctuation marks. Whether we're reading aloud or silently, the expression we convey with our voice brings meaning to the story. Our expression helps us understand what is going on.*

" *Today I want you to bring this story to life with your voice. Think while you're reading! How do the characters feel? Are they happy, sad, angry, or scared? Is something exciting happening? Tell the story with your voice!*

LESSON FOCUS
Making It Real

Fluency and comprehension are interwoven. When we read fluently, the story comes to life and the meaning becomes clear. The reverse is also true—when we comprehend a text, we are able to read it fluently. Comprehension without fluency is difficult, at best, and it's hard to be fluent without comprehension! So we have to teach our students to be fluent and to comprehend, but the two can't really be separated. This lesson combines the two effectively.

Before reading: Choose a story your students have read before. This lesson works best with text that has lots of excitement or strong character emotions.

During reading: Conduct the mini-lesson. As students are reading silently and then discussing, provide support as needed. You may have a few students you want to hear read to assess their oral reading. Listening to their conversations is a great way to assess comprehension. Scaffold support by joining any discussions that lack depth and ask questions that encourage deeper understanding. Make notes about interesting comments to share when you pull your students together again.

After reading: Gather your students back together. Review the importance of reading expressively and fluently. Share any challenges and successes you heard as you were listening to partners' discussions.

You will work with a partner today. You and your partner will reread a page or two silently. While you are reading, think about the meaning. When you've both finished reading the section, you will discuss the expression you think your voice should convey and why. Talk about what's going on in the story. How can you convey it with your voice? Let's do this first page together. Read it silently, and then we'll discuss how we should use our voices to bring the text to life!

Next, encourage students to explain what's going on in the text that makes them think they need to express it the way they did. For example, instead of a student simply saying he should read it to sound sad, ask him what's happening that makes a sad tone appropriate.

Now, what we just did together I want you to continue doing with your partner. Do your best to convey the author's story. I'll listen to your conversations. When you've finished discussing the page, take turns rereading it with good expression. Then do the same with the next page.

As you listen to partners discussing text, make notes about interesting comments you hear to share when you pull your students together again.

Sample mini-lesson

" *Who can tell me what it means to be a fluent reader? Does it mean speed-reading? No! Being a fluent reader means I can read like I talk. I have good expression, a natural pace, and I read with meaning. I tell the story with my voice. We know how punctuation helps us, so we already have a head start. I'm going to read a paragraph out loud a couple of times. After each reading, tell me if I sounded fluent and why or why not.*

Read slowly with poor phrasing; ask students why your reading wasn't fluent. Reread the passage quickly in a monotone, ignoring punctuation; again have students discuss your read-ing. Finally, reread the material with expression, natural phrasing, and a good pace.

" *Now that we know what fluent reading should sound like, you'll have a chance to practice it in your own reading.*

" *I'll set the timer for one minute and read to my partner. He will follow along on his sheet and lightly cross out any words I miss or skip. He'll cross them out lightly because I will be reading this three times, and he'll need to erase the*

LESSON FOCUS
Practice Makes Fluent

A rubric can be a valuable tool for students to use to rate themselves as readers. For this lesson, students will use a form to chart their reading rate and a rubric to evaluate their fluency. This lesson can be repeated monthly, and students can chart their progress on the reading rate record.

Before reading: Each student will need a copy of the *Reading Rate Record* on page 133, one copy of the *Fluency Rubric* on page 134, and a copy of the passage to be read. In addition, make overhead transparencies of the Reading Rate Record and the Fluency Rubric for explaining how each is used. We usually copy one or two pages from a book at each student's level and place the word count at the end of each line. For example, if the first line of text has seven words and the second line has six words, we write seven at the end of line one and thirteen at the end of the second line.

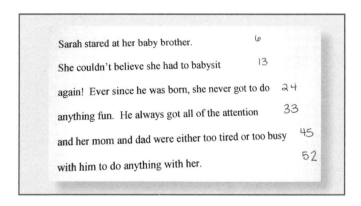

For this activity to have value, students must understand what they need to do to score well. Before beginning the lesson, go over the Reading Rate Record with your students and explain how they will chart their progress. It's very important to stress that this is not a competition and to review the rules for good reading-partner coaches (see page 45).

lines before I reread it. When the timer rings, he'll draw a line after the last word I read. To score the word count, I just look at the end of the last line I read for the total word count. Then I subtract any words I skipped or read incorrectly. This number is my words-per-minute score. Find where the number would be in the left-hand column on the record sheet and write it in the column under today's date.

Model each step on the transparency, allowing time for students to ask questions.

" *Fluency isn't just about reading words correctly, is it? So next, I'll use the Fluency Rubric to score my expression and phrasing. For expression, I'll think about whether I really made the story come to life with my voice. Did I read the punctuation correctly? I will give myself a 1, 2, or 3 depending on how well I think I read.*

" *I also want to think about my phrasing. Did I sound choppy or read "word-by-word," or did I read with some phrasing? Did I read with good phrasing all the way through? I will score a 1, 2, or 3 for phrasing as well.*

Demonstrate each step using the transparency and allow time for students' questions.

" *Now my partner reads to me. Remember, our goal is not to compete with anyone; it's to improve our own reading each time. Be more expressive, think about your phrasing, and your fluency will improve!*

During reading: Each student reads her passage three times. Set the timer and tell students when to begin. Circulate to help those having trouble scoring. When the Reading Rate Record has been filled in, partners switch roles. Continue until all students have read the passage three times, or until you run out of time. Collect these to save for the next time you'll have students do this. We always record their first words-per-minute score because it is important to know what the student's rate is when the material is unfamiliar, but you may prefer to record the final score.

The rubric for fluency is the next part of this lesson; you can also use it in another, separate lesson. Students rate themselves using this rubric. You can have them do this on their own, or with collaboration from their partner. If you are listening to a child read for fluency, your name would go on the line for partner. The value of this form is not so much to gain an objective view of each student's fluency, although you can use it to rate individual students as you listen to them read. Rather, it makes students aware of their expression and phrasing and helps them to focus on these characteristics of a fluent reader.

_____ s Reading Rate Record	Date	Date	Date	Date	Date	Date	Date	Date
Words Per Minute								
120+								
110-119								
100-109								
90-99								
80-89								
70-79								
60-69								
50-59								
40-49								
30-39								
20-29								
10-19								
0-9								
Phrasing Notes:								

Fluency Rubric

Reader _____ Partner _____

	1st Reading	2nd Reading	3rd Reading
Expression and punctuation	1 2 3	1 2 3	1 2 3
Phrasing Word by word 1 Some phrasing 2 Good phrasing 3	1 2 3	1 2 3	1 2 3

After reading: After you have collected the sheets, share some of your observations with your students. Give special attention to praising partners who worked well together.

LESSON FOCUS
Mystery Punctuation

This lesson serves two purposes. Students get more practice applying the information on the punctuation chart used earlier. More importantly, your students have to think in-depth about the meaning of the text in order to decide what punctuation marks belong there. By analyzing the text for the author's intent and thinking about what punctuation will help that intent come through, your students will internalize sophisticated comprehension strategies that they will be able to apply to every text they read.

Before reading: Choose a few pages of text that have plenty of different punctuation marks. Make one copy of these pages, white out all of the punctuation marks on the copy, and number them where they appeared in the text. For example, if the first mark is a comma, you would white it out and replace it with the number 1. Next, make copies of these pages with numbers in place of punctuation marks for each of your students. Prepare an answer sheet for students to record their responses. If you numbered 15 missing marks of punctuation, then you'll need to number the answer sheet from 1 to 15 and make a copy for each student.

Sample mini-lesson

66 *Let's review our punctuation chart (see page 132). We know an author uses punctuation to help tell the story and to bring his characters' thoughts and feelings to life. Today you're going to read part of a story that does not have punctuation. You'll work with a partner to decide what punctuation marks the author probably used. You and your partner have to be able to tell us why you chose each punctuation mark. What's going on in the story that makes you think the author would have used that punctuation mark?*

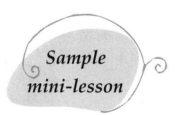

"Dad①where are my soccer shoes②" asked

Mark③

"They are wherever you took them off,"

his dad said④ "I'm not helping you find

them this time⑤"

Mark looked everywhere but he couldn't

To do this, partners will need to do lots of rereading and really think carefully about what would make the most sense. Each place that needs a punctuation mark is numbered. So, for example, when you figure out what punctuation mark belongs where the number 4 is, you will write that mark on your answer sheet next to number 4. Who would like to be my partner and model what to do?

Model this process with the first missing punctuation mark. Let students hear your thinking and your partner's thinking as you collaborate to figure out the missing mark. In addition, model the process of rereading the sentence to make sure the punctuation mark you've agreed on helps the text make sense. Let them see you or your partner recording your response on the prepared answer sheet.

During reading: After you've presented the mini-lesson, pass out the prepared text and answer sheets. Assign partners. As partners are reading and analyzing the text, scaffold your support based on individual students' needs.

After reading: Gather your group back together and go over the selection. Discuss differences in answers, making sure to have students explain their choices. There may be more than one correct answer, but as long as students can support their answers with solid reasoning, you've accomplished your goal.

Thinking about the types of punctuation marks an author uses to convey her meaning will also help students to become aware of punctuation in their own writing.

LESSON FOCUS
Fluency with Poetry

Poems present a special challenge to fluency instruction. They're fun for children to read, but to read them well students must tune into the clues the poet gives about how the poem should be read. These include punctuation, rhyme, and rhythm. Poetry offers great fluency practice; use it often to enhance your instruction and to develop fluent readers.

Before reading: Choose one long poem or two shorter poems at a level appropriate for your students. Copy your selections on large chart paper or create transparencies for the overhead. Also make a copy for each student.

During reading: Partners will practice reading fluently. Remind them to be expressive and make the poem fun to hear. When partners have both read it once all the way through, they can read it again, taking turns reading each line.

Poetry offers great fluency practice.

Sample mini-lesson

" *When you think of poems, what do you think of? Yes, most poetry we read rhymes, although not all poems do. Are poems fun to hear? Let me read you one of my favorite poems by Shel Silverstein. It's called "Sick." Have you heard it before?*

Read the poem with poor phrasing, paying no attention to rhythm or rhyme.

" *What did you think? Did you like the way I read it? What's it about? Was it kind of hard to understand the way I read it? Okay, let me try again.*

Read the poem again fluently, with good intonation, rhythm, and rhyme.

" *Did that sound better? Was it easier to understand this time? What did I do differently? You're right! I read it with more expression! You know how we've talked about clues writers give us to help us know how to read their work? Well, poets do the same thing!*

Poems usually have a special rhythm, kind of like songs. The poet has to choose and place his words and punctuation carefully, so the reader can find the rhythm. When a poem rhymes, the rhyming word or phrase is usually at the end of a line. When you read the poem, you need to emphasize the rhyming word to help the rhythm of the poem come to life.

I'll read the first few lines again. Listen to what I do with my voice to emphasize the rhyme at the end of each line.

Reread part of the poem.

Did you hear how that helped to create a rhythm?

I have chosen another poem for you to read today. Our goal as always is to bring the writer's message to life. Let's really tune into the clues the poet gives us to create the rhythm she intended. First, I want you to read the poem silently and look for the clues. Is it a rhyming poem? If so, what do you need to do to hear the rhymes?

Assign the reading, and after students have had time to read the poem silently, engage them in a discussion of the poet's clues.

After reading: After students have practiced reading the poem several times, call them back together and ask volunteers to read it fluently. Then ask students to share what they did to read the poem the way the poet intended. List their effective strategies and post them on a chart to refer to during independent reading.

Your chart might include:
- Stressed the rhyming words
- Paused at the end of stanzas
- Paid attention to punctuation
- Added expression that conveyed meaning.

Teacher Tip

Anytime your students are reading poetry or even writing their own poems, refer them to the same chart. Encourage them to think about these strategies whenever they encounter poetry.

Chapter 5

Questioning

Every two-year-old we know learns about her world by asking the same question over and over: "Why?" Think about how many times you have heard a young child ask this simple question. Our brains are natural questioning machines. Questions lead to understanding in all situations in our lives. When we drive down the street and see a new building, we immediately wonder what business is coming. Questioning is automatic and necessary to understand the world around us.

Questioning as we read is just as important. Next time you read something, pay attention to the questions your brain automatically asks and notice how those questions help you stay engaged with the text and understand it. The questions readers have before, during, and after reading set a purpose for reading, keep their minds involved in the story, and activate interest to engage them in the text. It is important for our students to learn to listen to the questions

their minds ask when they read and learn how to respond to these questions.

The lessons in this chapter encourage students to listen to questions their brains are asking and to use them to gain a deeper understanding of the text. By carefully modeling your own questioning process for them, you will teach your students how to ask important questions when they are reading. They will learn to ask deeper, more critical questions rather than superficial, literal ones.

Good Readers Ask Questions

People ask questions all day long. Asking questions helps us make decisions in our lives. Effective readers constantly ask themselves questions to clarify their thinking. When you introduce this strategy to kindergarteners or first graders, you may want to use the term "wondering." For example, "What are you wondering about this story?" This word is more natural to them and eases them into the strategy of questioning. Students need to question before, during, and after they read to keep their minds actively involved in the story.

Before reading: Choose any type of story for this activity. A big book that everyone can see works well; you can also give each student a small copy. In addition, you'll need a sheet of large chart paper divided in half vertically with the headings "Wonderings" or "Questions" on the left and "Answers" on the right.

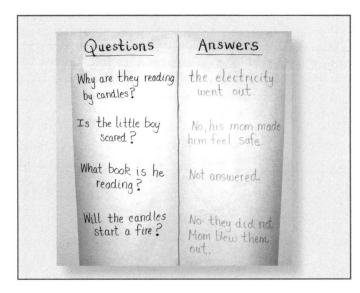

Sample mini-lesson

" *Today we are going to practice a strategy that will help us keep our minds in the story. It's called questioning. How many of you woke up this morning and wondered, "What am I going to wear today?" or "What's for breakfast?" What other questions did you ask yourself before coming to school?*

" *We ask questions all day long. I know when I drive, I am constantly wondering what the other driver will do. I need to be able to decide what to do to be safe on the road. Questioning is very important! For instance, if I wasn't a good swimmer, I might question how deep the pool was before I decided whether it would be safe for me to swim. Our brains keep us actively involved in our lives by questioning all the time.*

" We can use the same process when we read. In fact, good readers question before, during, and after they read a story to help them understand what they are reading. I'm going to read this book to you, and I'll wonder aloud as I read. I will also ask you to help me. We'll write our questions on the chart. Then when we finish reading, we'll see if our questions were answered.

During reading: Present the mini-lesson. Before you read, wonder aloud about what is going on in the cover illustration and ask questions about the title. Take a picture walk through the book and share questions that pop into your mind. As you read, invite the children to ask questions and record these on the chart. At this point, don't worry if their questions aren't important to the story. You'll teach good questioning in another lesson. It is important, however, that as you share your questions you think aloud about how they help you to understand what you read. Read the story to students.

After reading: Review the questions that were recorded and discuss whether any of them were answered. Invite students to raise their hands if they know the answer to a question. Ask them to tell you where in the story the answer can be found.

Remind students that whenever they read, they should notice questions their brains are asking. If they don't hear any questions inside their heads, they should reread to make sure their brains haven't taken a wrong turn.

More and More Questions

Good readers ask questions naturally as they read. To help beginning readers become aware of this thinking process, we have to teach the strategy explicitly. The frustration for many teachers arises from the types of questions students often generate—they just aren't important to the story. Give your students examples of questions that relate to the important parts of the story, as well as examples of questions that are irrelevant. The types of questions your students ask will give you insight and an instant assessment. Do they understand what is important in a story (main idea), or are they focusing on unimportant details? If students can generate good quality questions that show an understanding of the text, encourage them to move to the next level: engaging in critical discussions of the text.

Before reading: Choose a book at the appropriate level for your group. Determine one or two places in the text where students will stop and record questions they had while reading. Have sticky notes ready to give to students.

During reading: After conducting the mini-lesson, introduce the book you have chosen, modeling how you focus your brain and ask questions before you even start reading. Then read the first few pages with students reading along silently or with whisper voices. Invite students to share questions they have about the book. Record these if you wish and revisit them after the reading.

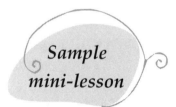

Sample mini-lesson

" *Questioning is something our brains do automatically whenever we focus on anything. For example, if a student went running across the room, I bet you'd focus on that student and your brain would start questioning like crazy! What's the matter? Why is she running? Is she upset? Will she get in trouble? If you're not focusing attention on that student, your brain won't wonder anything.*

The same thing is true when you read; if you're focusing on the text, your brain will ask questions. Questions help us understand and make sense of something. But the questions need to be relevant. That big word just means they need to be important questions. For example, if a student just ran across the room, and I wondered where she got the red shirt she's wearing, am I focusing on what is important? Will that question deepen my understanding of the situation? No, it would mean I had lost focus. I'd be missing the most important thing—a student is running in the classroom! We are going to really tune into our brains today and focus on our own questions. Are you ready? Let's do it!

Instruct students to read to the first stopping point and remind them to pay close attention to their thoughts. Give each student three sticky notes to record three questions they have as they read. They should leave the sticky notes on the page where each question occurred. While students are reading silently, assess reading and provide support as needed by having one student at a time "whisper read" to you. Give feedback on their questions, redirect those who are asking unimportant ones, and share your own text questions. Remind them that if they're having trouble thinking of questions, it means they are not focusing and they need to reread.

After reading: When most students have reached the stopping point, discuss the process with them. Ask if they were surprised by how many questions they had. Encourage students to share a question they had and discuss these, asking students to refer to the part of the text that made them ask the question. Remind them to tune into their questions every time they read.

Asking Important Questions

Some students will continue to struggle to ask questions that focus on the important parts of a story. You can group them together and teach this lesson. Students who comprehend only at the surface level have trouble with questioning; give them plenty of support and practice applying this strategy successfully.

Before reading: Choose a story your students are familiar with. It can be a book you have previously read to them or one that all students know. You will not be reading it to them, just reminding them of the story. Think of questions that pop into your head about the story. Make sure some of the questions are important ones, while others are unimportant to the understanding of the story. Write these questions on slips of paper, fold them, and place them in a jar. In addition, choose books to read to your students so they can practice applying this strategy with you.

During reading: Read a book to your students, stopping after every couple of pages to discuss questions they are having. Go through the process described in the mini-lesson, discussing whether or not each question would help them better understand the text. Share some of your own questions as you read to model the process.

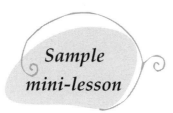

Sample mini-lesson

" *Today we're going to continue focusing on the questions our brains ask as we read. What are we wondering? What questions pop into our brains as we read? Remember, when we focus on what we're reading, we will have questions. Important questions will help us understand what we are reading. If you are not really focusing, or you're not focusing on what's important, your questions will reflect that.*

Remember the story "The Three Little Pigs"? I have written some questions that you might have had when you read that story. Some of my questions are important and some are not. Let's take turns drawing a question out of the jar. Our job will be to decide if the question would help us better understand the story. In other words, if we found the answer to that question in the text, would we understand the story better?

Now that we have a good handle on the kinds of questions that can help us understand a story, we're going to read a book together and tune into our questions. Remember, if we find we are asking questions that are not really important to the story, we are not focusing and we should reread.

You may want to record the questions on a chart to discuss after you have read the book. Ask students if their questions were answered. If so, did the answers help students to better understand the story?

After reading: Remind students to tune into the questions their brains are constantly asking. Also remind them that if they are asking questions that are not really important to the story, they are not focusing and should reread. You'll want to provide further practice and support for these students during silent reading. Try having them tune into their questions while reading silently and let them jot down questions on sticky notes. When you conference with them, discuss their questions.

Here are some sample questions you might include with this story.

What is the wolf's name?

Will the straw house be strong enough?

How does the wolf blow so hard?

Will the other pigs help the pig with the house of straw?

How many bedrooms do the houses have?

Why didn't the pigs all build a house together?

I wonder if the wolf will eat the pigs.

Which pig is the oldest?

Turn-and-Talk Questions

Learning to hear the questions our brains are asking while we read is just the first step. The next step is to think about those questions. Having your students discuss their thinking and their questions will not only increase their comprehension but also help them realize the importance of thinking more deeply about questions as they read. The purpose of asking questions is to help us better understand, but simply asking them is not enough. We need to try to answer them.

Before reading: Briefly review the purpose of questioning. Choose texts for your students and select a stopping point. You'll also need sticky notes for students to record questions.

During reading: Model what you want to see; choose a partner and read aloud a few pages of the book you've chosen. Think out loud as you ask and record a couple of your questions. Then, turn to your partner and begin a discussion. Encourage feedback from your partner and model how you accept all questions and thinking. There are no right or wrong answers. Model how your partner's thoughts and questions can cause you to think about the story in a new way.

Assign partners and the pages to be read. Give each student a few sticky notes for recording questions. When most students have reached the stopping point, tell them to turn and talk. While partners are discussing their questions, provide assistance as needed. If you see a really good discussion, or hear an example of a great question, make a note so you can remember to share it.

Sample mini-lesson

" *Remember our last discussion on questioning? Who can tell me why it is important for us to question as we read? Have you been tuning into the questions in your brains since the last time we met? Who would like to share an example? Remember, questioning is important; it improves and deepens our understanding. That's why we need to make sure our questions are important to the story. Don't get lost in unimportant details.*

Something else that deepens comprehension is discussion. One of my favorite things to do is to read a good book and then go to my book club to discuss it with my friends. We all bring our questions and thoughts and we discuss away! I learn so much from hearing what other people think. I always leave my book club with a deeper understanding of the story and with even more questions! In fact, sometimes I can't wait to reread the book. What we're going to do today is kind of like my book club. You'll read part of the story and record the questions you have. Then, you're going to meet with a partner and discuss each other's questions. Who would like to be my partner so we can model how a book discussion works?

After reading: End the turn-and-talk discussions while they're still going well. The first few times students do this, they may not be able to sustain a lengthy discussion. With additional modeling and practice, you'll see longer and more thought-provoking discussions. Share a few of the successes you observed. Ask students to share what was hard or did not go well and quickly brainstorm some ways to improve for next time. End the lesson by reiterating the purpose of questions and discussion, and how both can deepen understanding.

"Do Something Fast!" Questions

Now that you have introduced students to questioning and its purpose, and they've practiced tuning into their questions, it's time for the next step. There are different kinds of questions, and one of them signals confusion. Students need to pay special attention to these questions and respond immediately to them.

Before reading: This lesson reinforces the importance of metacognition. Students need to be aware of when they are confused and make a conscious effort to resolve the confusion. Remind them of the importance of keeping their brains on the road and noticing when they have slid off into a ditch and lost meaning. They will need to get their brains back on the road. This lesson will help them realize when one of their questions signals confusion and remind them of strategies they have learned to fix the problem fast.

During reading: Present the mini-lesson and then have students read an assigned portion of their texts. Remind them to pay close attention to all the questions they have and to really look for the confusing questions. With text at their instructional level, there should be opportunities to experience these questions. Tell them to make sure they look at the questions as emergency sirens that demand action. Read with a few students and have them ask their questions out loud. If you notice that they're making errors that confuse the meaning of the text, stop them and ask them if they understand what they have just read. Tell them that when they do not stop, it shows they are not yet active thinkers when they read.

Sample mini-lesson

" Now that we have learned about questioning and how asking important questions makes us better readers, we're ready to focus on another type of question. The questions we've focused on so far have been discussion questions relating to the story. However, there is another type of question that is just as important. I call these confusing questions. They are like a siren going off in your head—you have to do something! These questions mean you don't understand what you read; it isn't making sense. Well, if you don't do something, you will be lost. The purpose of reading is to understand, so if you are confused do something fast! This is another part of metacognition. You have to be able to recognize when you don't understand. Listen to your thoughts.*

Model this type of question by reading something aloud and showing that you're confused ("What does that mean?" or "That doesn't make sense" or, simply, "Huh?").

" *Did you hear my confusing question? Should I just ignore it and keep reading? Why not? Okay, what should I do? Yes, one thing I can do is reread. I can also read ahead a little, stop, and think about the story to see if my confusion has cleared up. Those are great strategies! If those don't work, and you're reading with a partner or with me in reading group, discuss your confusion. Sometimes just talking about the story can clear up this type of question. Remember, the most important thing is to watch out for those questions, to tune into your thinking, and to know when you don't know!*

After reading: Have students share some examples of the confusing questions they had, what strategies they tried to fix the problem, and how these helped. Remind them to use this strategy whenever they are reading.

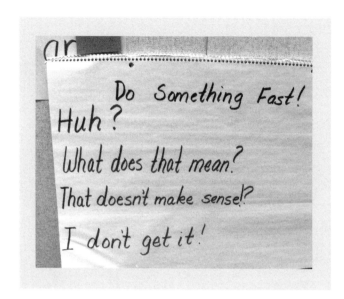

Chapter 6

Main Idea and Supporting Details

S tudents must be able to determine what is important when they are reading both fiction and nonfiction. The lessons in this chapter provide students with practice tuning into the author's message. These strategies complement all other strategies. As students are connecting, inferring, and visualizing, we always want them to focus on the important ideas or themes of the story or text.

What's the Big Idea?

This lesson is geared to younger children who are just being introduced to the concepts of main idea and supporting details, but it's also a quick review for older children and struggling readers. One way to make it easier for children to understand these concepts is to simplify them. We like to bring in a picture from home; children love learning about their teacher's life. In this example, the teacher has brought a picture of her son playing fetch with the family dog.

Before reading: Choose books at your students' instructional levels. Prepare an enlarged copy of the *Main Idea and Details* chart on page 135 and display for all students to see. Gather the children where they can easily see the photo you plan to share.

During reading: Support students who are having trouble making predictions. Ask questions to help them notice important information. For example, ask them what is happening in an illustration. Have them read the title to you. Ask them what clues the title provides.

Depending on the age of your students, you may want to use a big book to do a main idea and details graphic organizer together. With a picture book, you might have students preview the book if you don't think it will give too much of the story away. Older children can preview the book by reading the back and looking through it quickly. Students who are reading chapter books should look to see if the chapters have titles that might offer clues.

Sample mini-lesson

" Girls and boys, I brought in a picture of something that happens at my house all the time. What do you see? That's right. It's my son, Evan, playing ball with our dog, Dixie.

" What's going on in this picture? What is the main thing you see? Evan is playing fetch with Dixie; you're right! Evan is smiling and throwing the ball. Dixie looks like she's ready to chase it. So, if you were going to tell someone what was in my picture, what would you say? Sure, you would say I brought in a picture of my son playing ball with our dog. Isn't that the most important idea here? That's called the main idea. Let's put this photo in the main idea part of my chart.

We can notice other things in this picture. Let's take another look, and tell me what else you see. Yes, they're in my backyard. Right—it looks like it's warm outside because Evan is wearing shorts and he looks hot. Those are called details; I'll write those ideas under details on our chart. They aren't the most important things in this picture, but they do give us more information about the main idea. They help to tell the important story.

Just like my picture, stories have main ideas and details. The author has a main story line or reason for writing his book. The details in his story help bring that main idea to life. It is important to know what the main idea is when you are reading. The details are important too, but with my picture, for example, if you told someone I brought in a picture of a hot day in my backyard, you'd be missing the whole story!

Now, let's try this with your books. Look at the covers and try to predict what the main idea will be. When you have made a guess, write it in the main idea part of your organizer. Next, think about why you guessed as you did. What did you notice that helped you predict what the main idea might be? Now, look again. What interesting details might be included in your book? Record your predictions under the details heading of your organizer.

Main Idea and Details

Name Kai

Main Idea: _____

Evan is playing ball with our dog, Dixie.

Detail:	Detail:	Detail:
It's warm outside. He's wearing shorts and he looks hot.	They look like they are in the backyard.	It might be summertime.

After reading: Have students share their main idea and detail predictions. Remind them that when they have read the story, the author will expect them to understand the main idea. If the main idea is not understood, the story is not understood. Next, students will read their books to see if their predictions were close. If you are running short on time, you may have them read the books the next day after reviewing their predictions. Discuss whether their details supported their main idea. If students have differing opinions on the main idea, discuss these. The best learning usually comes when students try to explain their thinking and listen to each other's ideas. After students have read, discuss how making predictions helped them stay on track in their reading and focus on what was important.

Story Elements

Story elements are generally easy but still necessary to teach. You can teach each element separately, but teaching them together helps students get the big picture. The story elements create a map that helps them find their way to the main idea. You have already taught them to keep their cars on the road; the story map tells them the right roads to take! Begin by making it simple and visual for your students; they will have a much easier time understanding and remembering the elements.

You might use a situation that has happened in your classroom to introduce story elements. It can be as simple as a story about a child forgetting her lunch and how she solved the problem, or a story about a student new to your classroom and how he made friends. Many problems come up during the school day; just turn one into a little story.

The setting is easy for students since the story happens at school. The characters are memorable because your students actually know them, and the problem and solution aren't difficult to figure out because students have experienced them personally! Children like to see their names in the story, so try to come up with a problem in which everyone was involved. Make sure you don't use an incident that may embarrass someone.

Before reading: On chart paper or on the board, draw a square divided into four sections. Label each section with a story element: characters, setting, problem, and solution. Fold

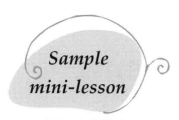

a piece of paper into fourths and write the story elements in the boxes. Make enough copies for your students. They'll work with a partner for this lesson.

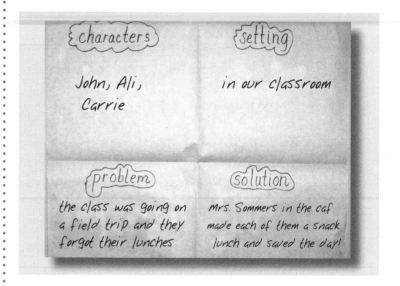

I want you to look at my chart. Who can read the four words on it? Yes; characters, setting, problem, and solution. Most fiction stories you read will contain these four elements.

In fact, most situations that occur in our classroom contain these elements. For example, remember last week when our hamster got out of its cage? Well, that's a story too! Let's retell that story and think about our four story elements. The main character is easy, isn't it? Let's write "Harry Hamster" in the box that says "characters."

Have students retell the story. Discuss each element and list it under the corresponding heading on your chart.

Now, I'm going to remind you of another story that happened in our classroom. I will tell you the story; be really good listeners because when I get done, you will work with a partner to figure out and record the characters, setting, problem, and solution of this story on your graphic organizer.

During reading: Discuss the meaning of each element and let students offer examples of each one from books they have read or movies they've seen. Then, tell the story you've decided on, assign partners, and give each pair a copy of the story element chart.

Scaffold support as needed while partners are working together to fill in each box on their graphic organizer.

After reading: When most partners have recorded the four story elements, gather them back together. Review each element, inviting partners to share their ideas. Discuss the importance of story elements and explain that the parts of a story make a map and help us keep the important information organized in our heads as we read.

Heads Up for Headings

Teach this lesson with any nonfiction book that contains headings. It is especially effective to teach this with the students' own social studies or science textbooks.

Before reading: Choose nonfiction books with headings; make sure they are at an appropriate instructional level for your students. Make a copy of the graphic organizer *Nonfiction: Set a Purpose for Reading*, on page 136, for each student. It's also a good idea to make an overhead transparency so all students can see the chart as you are explaining it.

During reading: Show students the graphic organizer and explain that before they read, they will record each heading and then think about it. They will write a question that the heading makes them wonder about, or predict something that might be in that section. Next, they will read the section and record whether their question was answered, or if their prediction was correct. If their question wasn't answered or their prediction wasn't correct, they should write one fact they did learn that was important in the section.

Do the first section together and model what you expect them to do independently.

Have students practice this process with two or three sections, providing support to those who need it. Try to keep students' questions and predictions relevant, modeling this repeatedly. Many times students try to get by with a very generic question. For example, if the section heading is "How Money Is Made," they can't just write, "I wonder how money is made." Encourage them to go further and ask something like, "I wonder if coins are made in the same place as dollars?" or "I predict that money is made at banks."

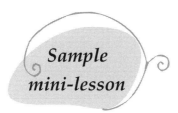

Sample mini-lesson

" *Nonfiction books are full of organizational tips we can use to be more efficient readers. One of these is headings; headings are like titles. They tell us the subject or the topic of the section we will be reading. Headings give your brain a focus and help you organize the information. The author puts a heading in a text for a reason: she wants you to know her purpose for writing. Before beginning to read the section, always read the heading. Then stop to think and ask yourself questions: What might you learn in this section? What does it make you predict or wonder about? Now you're ready to read, but in* a focused way because your brain already has an idea of what might be important.

" *There is no way you can remember everything you read, nor would you want to! However, you should be able to remember what is important. For example, if you are reading a book about money, and the first heading is "How Money Is Made," you might not remember all the information and details in that section. But you should be able to tell me how money is made! That was the whole reason the author wrote that section. When we read this book, we will make sure we use each heading to help our understanding.*

Nonfiction
Set a Purpose for Reading

Name _____Cameron_____

Record the heading and predict what you think you will learn about. Write one question the heading makes you wonder about. Read the section and then write what the section was about.

Heading ___What's Hiding Here?___

Prediction ___I think it is a lizard.___

Question ___How long does it take for lizards to change colors?___

What was it about? ___How some animals can use their colors___
___to hide from their enemies.___

Heading ___Weedy Sea Dragon___

Prediction ___Maybe it's about fish that really look like plants.___

Question ___Does it swim even though it just looks like a plant?___

What was it about? ___It said some fish hide in seaweed and___
___they can swim but not very fast.___

After reading: Have students share the predictions and questions they wrote prior to reading and discuss whether or not these were answered or confirmed. Ask them how this helped them organize their thoughts and tune into what was important in the sections. Remind them that this is something they should be training their brains to do whenever they read nonfiction books with headings.

Nonfiction Headings and Summarizing

Once students understand how headings are important tools for understanding nonfiction, they are ready to move on to the next step. The heading already gives them a "heads up" as to the content of the section. Now they're ready to use this focus to organize the main information in the section. This is a major step in learning to summarize effectively. You can teach this lesson with any nonfiction book that features headings. It makes sense to use the students' own social studies or science books. Because this is a higher-level skill, it will probably require many lessons for students to master. Take the time needed for students to master it, and you'll see the benefits in all areas of their reading.

Before reading: Choose nonfiction books that have section headings and are at your students' instructional level.

During reading: Do the first section together. Read the heading and stop to think. Question, predict, and wonder what the section might be about. Now read the section aloud to your students. Ask them to help you come up with one or two sentences that would really tell what the section is all about. Work together to make the sentences concise and accurate. Let students hear you trying to decide what is really the most important information. Discuss some ideas that are really just details and show them how you decided that they were not the main idea.

After doing one section together, have students follow the same steps for the next two or three sections. As they are working, listen to students read and provide support for

Sample mini-lesson

" *Let's review how headings help readers. They give us clues about what the author is going to tell us. Headings are kind of like titles for small sections of text. Skillful readers use them to help start their brains and begin thinking about what might come next. We did this when we predicted what a section would be about based on the heading.*

Now we are ready for the next step. Once your brain is focused and aware of what the topic is going to be, it's much easier to organize the information and tune into what's important. An author has a specific purpose for writing every section. You need to be a detective and pick up on the clues. There is no way you can remember every single fact in a nonfiction text—if you tried, you would go crazy. But if you're a skillful reader, you can easily remember the important ideas the author wants to convey. As you read the section, keep asking yourself what all the words are about. How do they relate to the heading? When you finish reading the section, stop and try to come up with one or two sentences that tell the main idea of that section. You don't want to retell everything in the section—just what's most important! Ask yourself if your sentence really tells what the whole section was about. Be careful—you want to be sure you aren't just picking up on one small fact or detail. Make sure your sentences are related to the heading. I am going to show you how to do this effectively with any nonfiction text that has headings.

using this strategy. You should also make sure each student's sentence or two is on target.

After reading: After most students have finished at least one section, stop and regroup. Ask students to share their thoughts about the process. What went well? What was harder than they thought it would be? Next discuss their summary sentences. Ask students to explain how they decided what was important.

When students learn to use headings to summarize nonfiction text, the benefits extend to all their reading.

LESSON FOCUS
Scanning

Scanning seems easy to us, but it is actually very difficult for our students. Scanning is a valuable tool that students will use throughout their academic years and beyond. Adults scan all the time. When was the last time you read an entire newspaper? Most of us just scan the headlines to find articles of interest. Think about Internet sites; we scan constantly when we search for information on the Web. Teaching your students to be purposeful, effective scanners will give them a valuable, life-long literacy tool.

Before reading: Choose nonfiction books at appropriate levels for your students. Again, you can use their science or social studies textbooks. Prepare questions ahead of time that students must use the texts to answer.

During reading: After presenting the mini-lesson, give each student a copy of the book you have chosen. Ask a question from the text and have students scan to locate the answer, and then raise their hands when they've found it. Call on a student to first answer your question and then tell you what clue word or words he found that helped him. The winner for each question earns a point. The person with the most points at the end wins.

You might also have students work in pairs for this game; the winning team could prepare game questions for the next lesson. This gives those students valuable experience thinking about important questions, too.

Sample mini-lesson

" *Have you ever been asked a question about something you've just read and you can't remember the answer? Have you ever tried to locate the answer to a question and you couldn't find it? Today we are going to begin practicing a reading tool called scanning. Scanning means to look through the text quickly in order to locate specific information.*

Now, if you were reading a book about polar bears and wanted to find out what polar bears eat, how would you go about doing it? You wouldn't need to read the whole book to find out. Instead, you would look quickly through the book for a place that makes sense for that information to be. That's what you do when you scan. Read the headings first and if you find one that might contain the information you are looking for, start scanning that section for important clue words. For example, if one heading is "Polar Bear Nutrition" and another heading is "Polar Bears and Their Babies," which section would you scan to find out what polar bears eat? That's right! The section with that clue word "nutrition" is where I would start scanning, too. I would move my eyes quickly over this section and look for words such as "eat" and "food." Maybe I wouldn't need to read the entire section. Let's try it! I have a book for us to practice with. I'll ask you some questions; let's see how quickly we can locate the answers.

Teach students to use headings in nonfiction texts to help them scan for specific information.

After reading: Review the steps on how to scan and explain when students would find this skill useful, such as during tests when they must read a passage and answer questions, especially when time is a factor. Scanning will also help them do research for reports effectively and efficiently. Create a chart with the situations in which students should remember to scan and post it in your classroom.

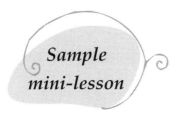

" *Has anyone learned how to play a new game recently? How did you figure out how to play? Did you read the directions or did someone tell you what to do? Here's another question: How many of you can remember playing a game and forgetting a certain rule or disagreeing about a rule with your friend? That happens at my house all the time when we're playing Monopoly! What do you think I do when that happens? Yes, I get out the directions. But if I had to read all the directions each time that happens, we would never get to play! So instead, I scan to find the place where that rule might be.*

" *Today you are going to do that. I have a copy of Monopoly directions for each of us. I am going to ask you questions about how to play the game. The first person to find the correct answer to my question gets a point. The person with the most points when time is called wins. Are you ready? Remember, game directions are nonfiction writing, so use the headings and clue words to help guide your eyes as you scan for the answer.*

LESSON FOCUS

Scanning Game Directions

An especially effective way to teach the why and how of a strategy is through an authentic situation students would actually use.

Before reading: Review the importance of scanning and when to use this strategy. Make sure to remind students how to scan by moving their eyes purposefully along a page as they look for a few key words. This will take practice for some readers—they will just want to read every word! For this lesson, you will need to find directions to a board game and make a copy for each student. We have used Monopoly, Yahtzee, Candyland, Chutes and Ladders, Junior Scrabble, and so on, depending on our students' reading levels. Even though the directions may be written at a higher reading level, students can still be taught to scan them for information.

During reading: As you are asking the questions, you can provide support to those students needing help. Some students may need help choosing the clue words to scan for. If you find the same student is finding the answer first each time, have her think of a question to ask the others to find.

After reading: Ask students to share some of the strategies they used when searching for an answer. Then brainstorm other situations for which this strategy would be useful, such as searching for an answer on a work sheet.

Chapter 7

Making Connections

Making connections is an important comprehension strategy that skilled readers use. It's a tool we need to give students to help them deepen their understanding of the text. Text-to-self, text-to-text, and text-to-world are the different kinds of connections students can make. Your students' understanding of each kind of connection individually is not as important as having them understand that any connection they make to the story increases their comprehension. Your goal is to teach students to use these connections to help them relate to the text so that they gain a deeper understanding.

We have separated the connections into the three categories commonly taught; however, teaching connections separately should be done only to familiarize students with the strategy. It is important to show them the different ways good readers connect with text, but it's really all about continuing to tune into their thinking as they read. After you have introduced connections, there's no need to separate them into categories. We want students to make connections naturally when they read and not worry about what kind of connection they have made. Comprehension strategies should help deepen understanding of the text naturally, so don't get caught up in the labels of text-to-self, text-to-text, and text-to-world.

Sample mini-lesson

" *You know that reading is all about understanding, right? One thing that helps us understand is when we can relate to something. For example, if I am reading a book about teaching, I can really connect to what the author says because I know about being a teacher. When we are reading a book, we need to be able to connect to it in some way before we can truly understand.*

" *Let's think for a minute about how we make friends. We often choose friends because we*

Text-to-Self Connections

Making connections and relating to the story you are reading is important for comprehension. Characters in books come to life when we can picture them in our minds from a connection we make. As you teach these strategies to your students, keep in mind the importance of meaningful connections. It's easy to spot a student who is not really applying the strategy and may not even comprehend the text. She will make connections that have little to do with the main idea of the story. For example, when reading a book about a little girl hiding under her bed because she was afraid she was in trouble, a student might make a text-to-self connection because she had a dresser that looked like the one in the picture! She was either not comprehending the central theme of the story or she was trying to force a connection and wasn't sure how to do it.

Before reading: Choose a short picture book to read to your students. Make sure it's one that you can easily use to make text-to-self connections. Before the lesson, gather together a basket of books at the appropriate level for your students. For older students, select a chapter from a book at their level. Students will also need several sticky notes each.

During reading: As you read to students, think out loud about the connections you are making to the text and to the illustrations. After reading, center the discussion around how your connections helped you better understand the story. Explain that when we can relate to a character or a situation, *have something in common. We have a connection. For example, one of my friends is a teacher, too, and we both love to read. Those two things give us a connection; we have them in common.*

" *The same is true with books. When I choose a book to read, I often select one that I have some sort of connection to. For example, the book I'm reading now is about a girl who is the youngest child in her family, and how being the "baby" affects her throughout her life. I have what's called a text-to-self connection with that book. I can relate to the character because I am the "baby" in my family!*

" *There are other ways we connect to books besides text-to-self connections like mine, when something about your life connects with something in the story. We can also make what we call text-to-world and text-to-text connections. We will talk about those later. Today we'll focus on text-to-self connections.*

" *First, I'll read you one of my favorite books. As I read, I'll let you hear my thinking. Listen for my text-to-self connections. Think about how they help me understand the story because that's why this strategy is important. Then we'll talk about my connections when I finish reading.*

As you read, think aloud about the connections you make. Discuss how they enhance your understanding.

" *I have a basket of books for you; look through them quickly and choose one you think you'll like. As you read, pay attention to your thinking. I'll give you several sticky notes, and when you find yourself making a text-to-self connection, write it on a note and leave it on the page where you made the connection. We'll share our text-to-self connections later.*

we can really understand how that character feels and what he thinks. The connection might even help readers predict what the character might do next.

As students are reading, listen to individuals read aloud. This might be a good time to take running records or anecdotal notes about your students' fluency and decoding strategies. Encourage readers to share their connections with you; discuss how these help them comprehend the story. Remember to steer them toward connections that relate to the important parts of the story. You'll see that students who are not really involved in a text will have connections with inconsequential story details, like what a character is wearing!

Text-to-self connections enhance comprehension.

After reading: After students have read for a while and you've had a chance to hold conferences with several students, ask volunteers to share some of the text-to-self connections they had and how these helped them to understand the text. End the discussion by reminding students why connections are so important: when we can relate in some personal way to what the author is saying, we can better understand the story.

Text-to-Text Connections

Text-to-text connections occur when our reading reminds us of something we have read previously. Text-to-text connections help students compare a variety of genres; they learn how to apply what they know about reading one type of text to help them read another type of text. Students may compare fiction and nonfiction, two different poems, a poem and a story, two different types of nonfiction, and so on. The connections they make between texts require critical, upper-level thinking skills as students analyze, contrast, and compare both texts for similarities and differences.

Before reading: Gather several different types of reading materials, such as a few different poems or several different nonfiction titles. Prepare copies of the graphic organizer *My Connections* on page 137 for your students and one as a transparency or enlarged chart version.

During reading: Present the mini-lesson. Fill out the graphic organizer on the overhead or enlarged chart, explaining to students what goes in each column. When students have been assigned partners and received their reading materials, work with pairs to provide support. Make notes of connections you hear that you want to share with the group at the end of the lesson.

Sample mini-lesson

" *My husband loves reading poetry, and the poems he reads are not easy to understand! Many times as he is reading, I hear him muttering. When I ask him what he's saying, he reads me part of a poem and tells me how it reminds him of another poem. Sometimes it's the message in the poem, and sometimes it's the rhythm of the words that remind him of another poem. These connections are how his brain analyzes the text to deepen his understanding. It shows he's a good reader because he takes the time to think about connections as he reads. Remember, it's thinking about the text that makes a reader skillful, not just saying the words!*

" *Today we will be making connections between different types of texts. For example, when I opened this book, I noticed a time line on page three. My brain made a connection to our social studies text. When we read about Abraham Lincoln, there was a time line of his life. That connection helps me know that I need to pay attention to this time line because it will probably give me important information I'll need to know as I read.*

You and your partner will select one text, and I will give each of you this three-column chart. In the left-hand column, write the words from the book that generated your connection. The middle column is for your text connections, and the column on the right is where you'll record how your connection helps you understand the text. With your partner, analyze the text and think. Have you read anything similar to this before? If it's a poem, does it rhyme? I bet you have read poems that rhyme. If you make a connection, write it in the middle column. Then in the column on the right, tell how that connection will help you read this text more effectively.

For example, noticing the time line and connecting it to our time line about Lincoln helps me know I will be reading about things that happened over time and the order they happened in. I'll refer to that time line often as I read.

So in the first column of my chart I'll write, "time line, page three." In the middle column I'll write, "social studies text, Abe Lincoln time line." And in the third column I'll write, "learned important facts about Lincoln." I will be sure to read this time line carefully to see what I can learn. Now it's your turn. I will be around to help and to listen to your discussions as you analyze the text.

My Connections

Name **Delia**

Text:	My text connection	How my connection helps me understand
Pg.# the polar bear has a thick layer of blubber. Blubber Blubber is in extra dark print	our social studies book has bold words	I can look for a glossary to see what the word means.
pg.23 The polar bear must find food or he will not survive the winter.	I remember that sometimes polar bears go into towns to find food.	There must not be many animals for the polar bears to eat.

After reading: Gather your group back together and invite partners to discuss their charts. Share any insightful discussions and great text-to-text connections that you observed. End the lesson by reminding readers to listen to their own thinking and to connections their brains make, and to use these connections to help them deepen their understanding as they read.

Text-to-World Connections

Text-to-world connections sound almost too complicated for our young students to grasp and even for us to teach. But text-to-world connections are just another way to take what we already know and understand and apply it to a text to help us deepen our understanding as we read. For example, if we know from our background knowledge the importance of recycling and its impact on our environment, we can apply that to a book we are reading about landfills to have an even deeper understanding of the issues involved. The key is to get our students to recognize what they already know that relates to what they are reading and to use that knowledge to add to and deepen their thinking as they read.

Before reading: Choose nonfiction books at your students' instructional levels. Look for topics that may already be familiar to them. In order to make connections, there must be background knowledge. If something is completely unfamiliar, making connections is much more difficult. It isn't necessary for your entire group to be reading the same text. You can even put a basket of different titles out and let each child choose one based on his interest. Select a book to read from to model for students how you start your brain, give it directions, and stop to think aloud about your connections to the text. Students will also need sticky notes.

During reading: Describe for students how your connections help you understand what you're reading. After they have had time to preview their chosen texts and activate

Sample mini-lesson

" *You always surprise me with how much you already know about so many things! And what you already know helps you understand new information when you read. For example, if I'm reading about a child whose father goes off to war, I can apply what I already know about the dangers involved, the bravery of soldiers, and how long people are away from home during wartime to help me understand the fear, sadness, and pride that child is experiencing. This prior knowledge of world events can help me take deeper meaning from the book.*

" *This is another way we make connections as we read. Since these connections happen because of each person's knowledge, we all have different connections. The key is to listen for the connections our brains make, and take time to think about them and what we now understand about the text because of our connections.*

" *Today you'll choose a nonfiction book. Before reading, do what good readers do. Start your brain and give it directions. As you read, listen for the connections to pop into your head. They may sound like this, "Oh I know something about . . ." or "I've heard of . . ." Give yourself time to think. Could this connection help you understand the book better?*

" *On your sticky notes, jot down connections you make; leave your note on the page where you had the connection. Later, we will discuss these connections and how they added to your understanding.*

their background knowledge, discuss any connections they might have had and how those connections might be useful to them as they read.

Being aware of what they are thinking as they read can be difficult for some students. They'll need plenty of opportunities to practice this and frequent reminders of how important it is. Provide support by listening to them read and letting them hear some of the connections you have while they are reading.

After reading: Gather the group back together and discuss the connections they had. After each connection is shared, focus discussion on how the connection helped deepen understanding of the text. If you find that many of your students have trouble with this strategy, repeat this lesson with another read-aloud, modeling your own connections to the text as they occur.

Teacher Tip

Nonfiction books about animals will facilitate teaching this lesson to younger readers. They can usually make connections to these texts easily.

Connections Overview

This lesson begins the final stage of teaching students about making connections as they read. Now that they are familiar with the three types of connections and how they help us to read, it is important not to focus on them separately. After all, it isn't how we actually read; we don't classify connections as text-to-text, text-to-self, or text-to-world mentally, or think about what kind of connection we have made. Making connections comes naturally to skilled readers; it just happens!

Before reading: Make copies of the *Many Connections* graphic organizer on page 138 for each student and have enough sticky notes on hand to give each student three. Choose a set of books at your students' instructional level.

During reading: Use this time to collect data on individual students, do oral reading assessments, and make anecdotal notes. Scaffold support to students as they are reading and recording their connections.

Sample mini-lesson

" *Today we are going to open up our minds to all types of connections. Let's review the three different kinds of connections we have learned about and practiced in our reading.*

" *Today when you're reading I'm not going to tell you what type of connection to focus on. Instead, I want you to record any connection you make. After all, we can't control when or what type of connections will occur. They just happen naturally as we are reading, as long as we have our brains tuned into the text.*

" *I'll give you three sticky notes. When you notice that your brain has made a connection, quickly jot it down with the page number where it occurred. Take a look at your connections chart. There are three columns, one for each kind of connection we've discussed. After you have written a connection on a sticky note, think about which kind it is. Is it a text-to-text, a text-to-self, or a text-to-world connection? Then, place the note on the chart in the column where you think it belongs. When we finish reading, we'll share some of our connections and talk about what kind each one is. I'll use tally marks to keep track of how many of each type of connection we have. I'm curious to see which kind occurs the most. Remember, you don't need to try to have all three kinds of connections. They occur naturally when you are tuned into the text. Happy connecting!*

After reading: One by one, have students share a connection, and allow the group to discuss where it should go on the connection chart. As always, center the discussion on how each connection helped the reader to understand the story better.

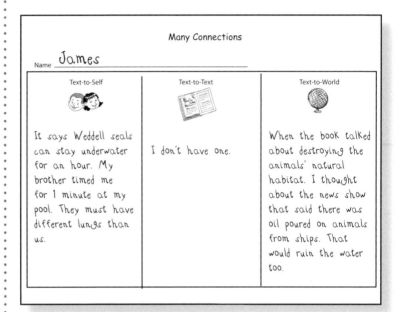

Another way to use this graphic organizer is to have students record their connections directly in each column as they are reading independently.

LESSON FOCUS

I Connect, So Now I Know

We know that effective readers make all kinds of connections to texts they read. But how does making connections really help us to be better readers? Making the connection is only the beginning; deeper understanding happens when we apply our connection and relate it to the text. If we are going to teach our students about making connections as they read, it is critical that we also teach them how to use their connections to enhance comprehension, which is, of course, our goal.

Before reading: You will need a set of fiction books at the appropriate level for your students. While we can connect in some way with almost any book we read, this lesson works especially well using a text with well-developed characters. Make enough copies of the graphic organizer **Connect to Understand** on page 139 for all your students and one as a transparency or an enlarged version to use for modeling.

Sample mini-lesson

" *Remember this book we read and all the interesting discussions we had about our connections? What were some of your connections? Now for the big question: why are connections so important when we read? Think about the connections you made. How did they help you understand the story? Be specific! Say, "My connection was . . . and it helped me understand . . . . "*

" *For example, I'm reading a book about a mom whose daughter is missing. Of course, this mom is terrified and very upset. When I read the part about her turning around in the grocery store and realizing that her little girl was missing,*

I had a major connection! I could feel myself getting upset because I have a daughter and I know how terrified I would be if she were missing! So to explain how this connection helps me understand this book, I might say, "My connection was when the mom lost her daughter because I have a daughter, and I'd be terrified, too. My connection helps me understand how upset and scared this character is feeling."

" *Look at this graphic organizer. The left side is where you'll record your connection. In the middle, write the page number where the connection occurred. On the right, record what your connection helped you understand. Watch how I record my connection.*

" *By becoming aware of your connections and taking time to think about the story based on your connection, you will understand on a much deeper level. If I was reading about two best friends, and one of them moved away in the middle of the school year, I would make major connections. I'd have a text-to-self connection because when I was younger, my best friend moved away. I was so sad and lonely! I can understand how the friend who is left behind feels. She'll have to make new friends and find someone else to sit with at lunch and play with at recess. Now I'm much more involved with the text. The author didn't need to tell me all these things; I know them through my own experience.*

" *Remember, you shouldn't worry about the kinds of connections you are making. Just record any connection that you make. Start your brain, give it directions, and enjoy the book.*

During reading: Present the mini-lesson and then scaffold support to those who need it. Many of your students will need help applying their connections to the text to deepen understanding. Provide support for this process by asking questions that focus their thinking.

After reading: Share your observations and discussions with students. Note the different connections students made, reminding them that because everyone's schema differs, there are many different connections. Discuss how some experiences are nearly universal, and almost every reader can identify with these, such as making new friends or losing a good friend who moves away. Ask volunteers to share some of their connections. Remind them to keep analyzing their connections for deeper meaning within the text.

	Connect to Understand	
Name **Trevor**		
My Connection	Pg#	What It Helps Me Understand
I was scared when I first saw how big my mom's friend's horse was.	7	She probably thinks the horse might hurt her and that's why she ran from him.
This boy at recess never thinks I'm good enough to play basketball with him.	12	She wants to show him she can be good at riding a horse.

Chapter 8

Visualizing: Bringing the Story to Life

Have you ever been disappointed in a movie that was based on a book you loved? For skillful readers, books are almost always better than movies because when they read, they make their own movies inside their heads. They can picture the characters, the setting, and the plot. To see those "mind pictures" altered in a movie changes the entire experience for book lovers.

All of our visualizations are unique because of our personal background knowledge or schema. When we visualize a text, we bring our previous experiences to it. Attend an adult book club and listen to the participants discuss their visualizations to see how true this is! From the way a character looks and speaks to the sights and sounds of the setting, our minds create vivid pictures. When we teach visualization to our students, there is no right or wrong model for the visuals they create. But their minds should be focused on what is important in the story. If their visualizations center around minor details of the story, you'll want to question their comprehension. We have designed these lessons to encourage your students to bring stories they read to life by picturing the author's words, which in turn leads to deeper comprehension.

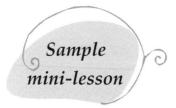

Sample mini-lesson

" *Boys and girls, what makes reading so great? Well, one thing I love about books is that they let you see, hear, feel, and almost experience something no matter where you are. Now, sometimes it's easy.*

Hold up the book with pictures.

" *I can tell you what I see, hear, and feel when I look at this page. What do you see and hear? How does this picture make you feel? What makes this so easy? That's right, pictures! The pictures help make this book come alive.*

Next, hold up the chapter book open to a page with no illustration.

" *Now, what about this book? What do you see and hear? You don't see anything? Hmm . . . maybe I have the wrong page. Let me try a different one. Now what do you see, hear, and feel? Why is this so much harder than it was with the first book I showed you? You're*

LESSON FOCUS
Do You See What I See?

As teachers, we struggled to find an effective and meaningful way to teach visualization, an important comprehension strategy. We saw it as something good readers do. However, when we focused on teaching it, our students seemed to have wonderful visualizations about the most inconsequential parts of a story!

We knew that visualizing aids comprehension and that our students would benefit from knowing how to do it. After many discussions about teaching visualization and if it was really necessary, we realized that it is worth teaching, but it needs to occur within another strategy: determining what's important. Students need to be able to tune into what's important in the story before they can have relevant visualizations. This doesn't mean that we think all visualizations should be the same, or that there is a right or wrong way to "see" in our minds what the author portrays with her words. What we came to believe as teachers of reading is that visualization enhances and heightens comprehension when the reader tunes into the author's main idea or message.

Before reading: This lesson introduces students to the why and how of visualization. Choose a book with pictures and a chapter book without pictures. Also select a book to read aloud and choose a place to stop in the middle of the story. When you stop, you will have students draw what they see in their minds. Make copies of the graphic organizer *Do You See What I See?* on page 140 for each student.

absolutely right. There are no pictures. But let me tell you—this author has worked very hard to draw pictures for you. She painted pictures with her words and even with the punctuation she chose. She has done everything she can to make this story come to life, but you have to do your part. You have to tune into what she is saying and to the story she is weaving. Then I promise you will see the book come to life!

" *We won't all see the same things in our minds when we read, even though we'll read the same words. The characters, the setting, even the way a character sounds and moves vary greatly in our minds. What will be the same, if we are really tuning in, is that we will all see the main idea of the story and what is really important.*

" *Let's practice this today. I'll read this book to you, but I won't show you any pictures. Instead, I want you to tune into the story and listen to all the author's clues about what she wants you to see. I am going to stop halfway through the story and give you a few minutes to draw what you see on this paper where it says, "I see . . . ." Remember, we want to focus on the main part of the story—what's most important. Then I will read the rest of the story and you can draw what you see at the end on the right side of your paper.*

During reading: Read the story to your students, being careful not to let them see any pictures. At the halfway point, stop and have them sketch their visualizations on their graphic organizers on the left side. Ask students to tell you about their drawings. Are they getting the important themes and ideas? Provide support to students who are focusing on unimportant information. Next, read the rest of the story and have students sketch what they now see on the right.

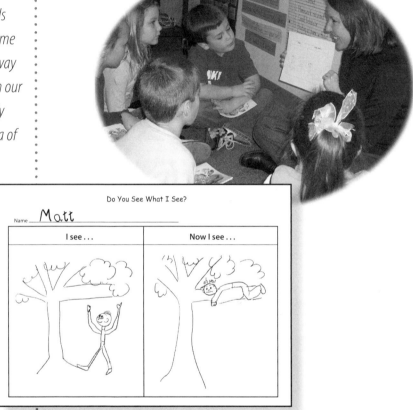

After reading: After students have completed their drawings, invite them to share what they drew. The most important part of this lesson is to have students relate their sketches to the text by asking them what in the story made them see what they drew. What did the author say that helped them see it that way? Remind them that visualization is important because it helps us understand and ties us into the text. We have to do what the author can't. We have to add sounds, moving pictures, colors, smells, and feelings.

Sample mini-lesson

As you continue teaching your students to maximize their ability to visualize, remind them often of the purpose. The author tells the story, but our minds bring it to life. We have found it helps to have students describe and explain the pictures in their minds. Let them hear from other students how their minds are picturing the story based on what the author wrote.

Before reading: Select books appropriate for your groups. Choose at least three stopping places in the text for students to stop and draw their visualizations. You may mark these with sticky notes prior to the lesson or write the page numbers on the board for students to refer to. Also make copies of the graphic organizer *My Visualization* on page 141 for each student, as well as a transparency for modeling how to use the organizer.

" *We have talked about the importance of visualizing and seeing the pictures in our minds. Today you are going to think about your visualizations as you read on your own. Remember, the author does her best to help us see the story; we just have to tune into her words.*

" *Look at this graphic organizer. On the left, you will draw your visualization. On the right, you'll record what the author said or what was happening that helped you to see that. Here's one from a book I read. Notice my first picture. I drew a girl with her hands up to her mouth and a huge smile on her face. The other person in the picture is her dad. On the right, where the text goes, I wrote, "Her dad told her she will finally get a horse of her own! She was so excited." This isn't the exact text, but it tells what happened and what was important. In my mind, I could really see how excited and surprised she was.*

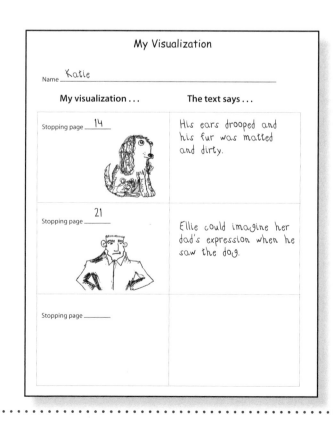

" In the next square, I drew her again next to a funny-looking horse. This time she's not smiling; she has tears on her cheeks. In the text square I wrote, "She is so disappointed and embarrassed; her dad actually bought her a donkey." Do you see how this works? Notice that I drew what was important in the story. Don't get caught up in drawing small details that were mentioned. Focus on the main message.

" Here is the book you'll be reading today. I have chosen three stopping points. The page numbers to stop at are on the board. Start reading, and when you come to one of the stopping points, do a quick drawing of your visualization. Then, in the text box, write what you read that helped you visualize your picture. For instance, if you draw a character laughing, next to the character write the words the author used or what was going on in the story that helped you to see that.

During reading: This would be a good time to listen to a few of your students read and also discuss their drawings as they are doing them. Encourage them to tell you what the author wrote that helped them to see their visualization. Make note of those students having a difficult time visualizing the important parts of the story. Then plan to group them together and teach more lessons on story mapping and determining what is important.

As they sketch, encourage students to tell you what the author wrote that helped them to see their visualization.

After reading: Share with your group some of the things you noticed as you were discussing the drawings with individual students. Give examples highlighting what the author said and the students' visual interpretations. If you find most of your students are having trouble, do a quick drawing and label yours with the author's words.

Turn-and-Talk Visualizations

This lesson encourages students to share what they see with a partner. It's interesting for them to hear what other students are visualizing and it helps them realize that while some of their visualizations may differ, the important parts of the story can still be seen. Turning and talking about their visualizations will also encourage your reluctant readers to really focus on the text as they read. Their peers will hold them accountable!

Before reading: Choose books appropriate to the level of your students. Before beginning the lesson, choose a short section of the text that has good, descriptive language and lends itself to visualizing. You will read this section to students.

During reading: After you present the mini-lesson, choose a student to be your partner, and read a short section of the book you've selected. Then stop to model the discussion that would take place. Make sure to model how good partners respond to each other's visualizations. Also, show students how you relate the visualizations back to the text by telling your partner what the author wrote that made you visualize what you did. Remind students that it is their background knowledge or schema that influences their visualizations and makes them unique. Having different visualizations is fine, as long as the visualizations show understanding of the story.

While partners are reading and discussing, provide support as needed. Be especially careful to note whether or not students are paying attention to what's important. If some are having difficulty with this, redirect them and perhaps plan to reteach the introductory lesson on visualization to them in a separate group. Make note of turn-and-talks that went well and share these with your group after reading. Also use your notes to plan further instruction on visualization.

Sample mini-lesson

" *You know, I thought about all of you last night. I was reading a book and I just felt like I was right there with the character. The author wrote so vividly that I was really able to see the story. I felt like I was in it! That's when I thought of you! I hoped with all my heart that you feel like this when you are reading a really good book. Because when you do, there's nothing like it! Have any of you had experiences like mine with a good book?*

" *Today we are going to continue the books we have been reading. But instead of stopping to draw your visualizations, you will work with a partner. You'll turn and talk with your partner to describe what you both are seeing. Make sure you also tell your partner what the author wrote that helped you visualize what you are seeing. Then talk about how both of your visualizations are alike and different.*

After reading: Praise partners who worked especially well together. Ask students to share how their partner's visualizations were the same or different and if that surprised them.

Turning and talking about their visualizations encourages reluctant readers to focus on the text as they read.

Where Was I?

This is a good way to encourage deep engagement in the text. The visualizations will be yours, but students will benefit from seeing how your mind works as you read and what causes you to form visualizations. Don't stress out if you're not an artist; in fact, quick, simple sketches work better here. We want our students to see that they don't have to be artists.

Before reading: Read the story yourself. Divide a sheet of paper into thirds and sketch a picture in each section of three events from the story. Make copies for students.

During reading: Conduct the mini-lesson. As students are reading, take this opportunity to listen to individuals read and encourage them to think aloud as they problem-solve where in the story your sketches came from. Make note of any students who seem to have a difficult time so that you can plan additional support and lessons for them.

After reading: Have students tell you where in the story your pictures belong and, most importantly, ask them for proof! If there are differing opinions, encourage discussion before you tell them the correct answers.

Sample mini-lesson

" *I have a challenge for you today. We have been focusing on visualizing the story the author tells. Today I want to see if you can match my visualizations to the appropriate parts of the story. I read the book we've been working on and drew illustrations of several visualizations I had while reading. I'll give each of you a copy of my sketches. Your job will be to read the book, match my sketches to the correct parts of the story, and tell me what the author said that proves you're right. I know these are my visualizations and of course, yours might be different, but to do this you'll really need to tune into the text. You will need to use your good brains to figure out when and why I had that particular picture in my mind. Are you ready for my challenge?*

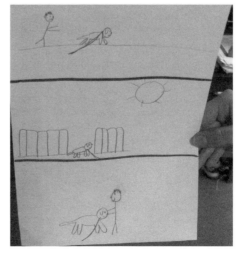

Illustrate three different sections of the book students are reading.

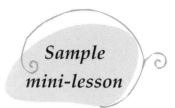

" *Are you ready for another challenge? Before we begin, I would like to ask you a question. I want you to really think before you raise your hand to answer, so no hands up for one minute! Here's your question: how does visualization help you to be a skillful reader? You have one minute of think time.*

" *Great! You really understand the value of seeing a story come to life. Let's focus on our visualizations again today. You will be working with a partner and using the books we have just finished. Here's your challenge. As you work with your partner, I want you to look through the book, reread a section to yourself, and then draw your visualization. Your partner will have one minute to find the part of the story you drew. Then you'll switch roles; your partner will draw a visualization from part of the book, and you'll need to try to find the correct spot in the story! You need to do a very quick sketch.*

" *Before you begin, let's try one together. I am going to draw one of my visualizations and then give you one minute to find it in the book. Ready? Go!*

LESSON FOCUS
Sketch and Scan

This is a good visualization lesson to teach when students have finished a book. It builds on the previous lesson. However, this time instead of you drawing and your students trying to figure out where you were reading, students will work with partners and take turns reading and sketching. As students attempt to find where in the text their partner's visualization fits, they will also be practicing the skill of scanning text. This lesson also requires rereading, which benefits fluency.

Before reading: For this lesson, each student needs blank paper and a pencil or a small dry-erase board and marker.

During reading: Conduct the mini-lesson. You may need to remind students to keep their guessing to a minute and to sketch very quickly. Work with any students who are having difficulty. Struggling readers especially may have trouble scanning the book to find the text that identifies their partner's visualization. These students tend to think they need to read every word to find what they are looking for. You'll want to group these students together later and provide more practice with scanning.

After reading: Share the successes and challenges you observed and invite students to share their own successes and challenges. Close the lesson by reminding students to use visualization whenever they are reading.

Chapter 9

Inference

*I*nference is a difficult strategy to teach, especially to struggling readers. It comes naturally to us, but it's hard for students to transfer the skill to text. We need to teach them that inferring is just using what they already know and combining that knowledge with what the text says to better understand an author's message. Just as with all the strategies in this book, explicit instruction and careful modeling are critical before our students can apply this strategy independently.

Teaching young readers to make inferences involves teaching them to think. They have to learn to use the information the author gives them and think about what assumptions, predictions, and conclusions they can make. If the situation in the book were happening to them, what would they be thinking? Predicting, drawing conclusions, and making assumptions all require that readers use their knowledge about life from their own experiences and apply it to the text to infer the bigger picture.

It All Adds Up

We make inferences constantly. We use clues from a situation, plus what we know, to make an inference. For example, if I am at the grocery store and see a person buying candles, a cake mix, wrapping paper, and ice cream, I can infer that it is someone's birthday. The clues are the items being purchased. My prior knowledge tells me that on birthdays people usually have cake with candles and ice cream. When I put these clues together, I infer that a birthday is involved. The same thing happens as we read. We take the clues from the text and combine them with what we already know to make inferences. We just need to teach our students how to do it.

Before reading: This lesson focuses on inferring characters' feelings. Choose books that have strong character interactions and are at appropriate levels for your groups. Select two stopping places that will give students an opportunity to use this strategy. Make copies of the **Do the Math** graphic organizer on page 142 for students, as well as a transparency if you plan to use the overhead.

Sample mini-lesson

" *When an author writes a book, he expects you to bring your background knowledge to the story. He expects that you will be able to take what he says and add your own experience to understand the story fully. This strategy is called making inferences or inferring. Think of it as a math problem: clues from the text, plus what you know, equal inference.*

Write the equation "clues from the text + what I know = my inference" on the board.

" *For example, if I'm reading about a person playing baseball and the author says the person struck out, I can use the clue from the text (struck out) plus what I know (striking out is not good) to infer that the character is upset! Easy, right? Let's try it. First, I want to show you this chart.*

" *There is a place for the clues from the text and a place for your own ideas. Then below those, you'll see a place to make your inference. Are you ready?*

First, I'll read you a paragraph I wrote about my children and our dog, Chester, and then I'll ask you what you can infer. Listen carefully.

Christopher and Emily came running around the corner and saw Chester. They were so relieved! Chester looked tired and he was panting! They raced up to him, grabbed his collar, and pulled him back to their house.

Now, what can you infer from this paragraph?

Possible responses include
- Christopher and Emily were really worried about their dog.
- Chester ran away.
- Chester got lost.
- Someone was chasing Chester.

What clue did you hear? What do you already know that helped you? Right! Christopher and Emily were running to find Chester. What you already know is that if you're worried about your dog, you'd be running to get him and you'd be very happy to find him. So we can infer that Christopher and Emily were really worried about Chester.

Now it's your turn to practice this strategy. I have selected two stopping points and written the page numbers on the board. When you come to each one, make inferences about how the character feels. Use the graphic organizer to explain your thoughts. Record the clues from the text and what you know that helped you come up with your inferences.

During reading: After presenting the mini-lesson, provide support as needed. Listen to individual students read and take notes about their fluency and accuracy. Scaffold support to students who may have trouble using the chart and making inferences. These observations will help you decide which students need additional support to learn this strategy.

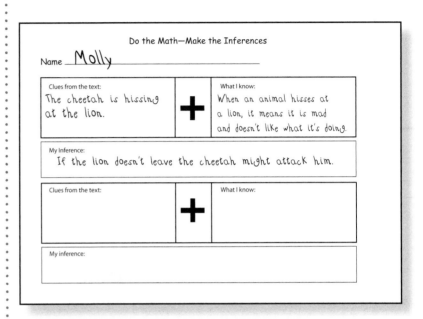

After reading: After most students have had time to read and make at least one inference, go over their graphic organizers and discuss the different inferences students have made. As always, make sure to focus their inferences on the text by having them explain both parts of the equation. They should be able to tell you what clues they found in the text and what they already knew that helped them reach their inference.

Sample mini-lesson

" How many of you are reading a text that has some challenging vocabulary words? All of us have at one time or another—for me it happens daily! Today we are going to work on what to do when we encounter a word we don't understand.

" Let's practice this skill. I copied a page from a book for you to read. Some of the words have been blacked out. Your job will be to use the words around the missing word and their meanings to figure out what the missing word could be. First we'll try one together.

LESSON FOCUS
Be a Word Detective

Every teacher knows how frustrating it is when a student misreads a word and the error makes absolutely no sense to the meaning of the text. Being able to infer word meanings is crucial, and it is a skill that must be taught explicitly.

Before reading: Before the lesson, choose a book at your students' instructional level. Copy one or two pages and black out several key words on these pages, and then recopy the pages. Make transparencies of them as well. In addition, you'll need two large index cards or pieces of oak tag. On one, write the word "march." On the other, write "My band teacher tells us to march to the music."

During reading: Discuss with your students what they do when they don't know what a word means. Try to get them to verbalize the steps they take to figure out the word's meaning. Ask them if they can get enough information to allow them to keep reading with understanding.

Then, hold up the card with "march" written on it and ask students to tell you what it means. Most likely, students will give you both definitions, the name of the third month and a way of walking. Tell them both meanings are correct and discuss how they can figure out which meaning to use if they see the word in a book.

Next, hold up the card that reads, "My band teacher tells us to march to the music." Ask them the meaning and discuss how they figured it out. Elicit that they used the words around the vocabulary word to figure out which "march" was meant. Praise their good thinking and remind them to do the same thing when they read.

Explain that you want them not only to figure out the meaning of the missing word but also to explain how they came to their conclusion. Be sure to tell them they really need to pay attention to and tune into their thinking.

Place the transparency on the overhead. Read to the first missing word and beyond to the end of the sentence. Give a minute or two of think time and then begin calling on students to tell you what the missing word might be and, more importantly, to explain their thinking. What went through their minds as they problem-solved the meaning of the missing word? They need to be specific!

As students are working, ask individuals to whisper what they think the next word might be. Make note of students who are having difficulty with this skill. You'll want to group them together for additional lessons.

If you want to, have students work with partners for this lesson; they can turn and talk about their thinking and try to agree on a possible word. Call on partners or individuals to share their answers and, most importantly, their thinking. Encourage students to compare the thinking and problem-solving that brought them to their answer.

After reading: Share some of the thoughts you had as you were listening to their thinking. Ask volunteers to tell you their suggestions for the missing words. Be sure to applaud and validate any and all answers that would work, as there may be more than one. Show your word detectives the real missing word. Remind them to use this strategy whenever they are reading and come to a word they do not know.

What Does It Mean?

Once you have introduced your students to the process of inferring word meanings, they are ready for the next step. This lesson builds upon the previous one by having students apply the strategy in a meaningful way to text they are reading.

Before reading: Choose a fiction or nonfiction text at your students' level. Look through the book and select three words they may have difficulty understanding. Make a copy of *What Does It Mean?* on page 143. Write one of the three words on each word line. Then make a copy for each student. Give a brief book introduction to activate prior knowledge and build interest.

During reading: Give students the graphic organizer and explain how to fill it in. Do an example with students, then assign the pages to be read. Read with individuals to check their understanding of how to use the strategy. Scaffold support to those students who need it and make notes for planning additional lessons for small groups.

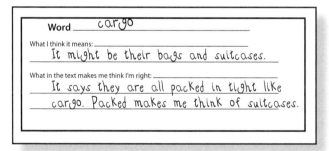

Word ___ cargo ___

What I think it means: ___
It might be their bags and suitcases.

What in the text makes me think I'm right: ___
It says they are all packed in tight like cargo. Packed makes me think of suitcases.

After reading: When students have completed the assignment, ask them to explain the thinking they used to figure out the words. If a student has a word that she couldn't figure out, invite other students to offer suggestions and tell why they think they are correct. Emphasize that encountering words you don't know does not mean you aren't a good reader or that you aren't smart—it happens to everyone! A smart reader realizes when she loses understanding and knows what to do to solve the problem.

Sample mini-lesson

" *Now that I have introduced our new book, I want to tell you about the thinking strategy we will focus on today. Last time we practiced being detectives to figure out the meanings of unknown words. Today, we're going to do the same thing, but this time they will be words in your book.*

" *Don't keep reading if you can't figure out the meaning! Remember, effective readers are actively involved in making sure they understand what they read. You will get to use this strategy several times while you're reading today.*

Sample mini-lesson

LESSON FOCUS
What a Character!

Character traits are important to teach. While it's easy to get caught up in character-trait terms (like honest, kind, or timid), the focus should always be on what the author says that defines a character. Remind students often that the character is in the words; their job is to be active thinkers who bring the character to life. These are easy but important lessons you can teach with any fiction text. Resist the urge to use character trait work sheets. Focus instead on encouraging students to become active thinkers, and use this lesson to teach them to be thoughtful readers.

Before reading: Choose fiction books at an appropriate level for your students. Make a copy of *What I Think About*, on page 144, for each student.

During reading: Assign the pages to be read and hand out the graphic organizers. As students are reading, have individuals read to you. Assess their use of strategies; your notes will help you plan additional needs-based mini-lessons. If you notice students are having trouble getting to know a character, model for them by sharing a clue you see from the story and how it drives your thinking about the character.

> *You know, an author has a tough job. He has to introduce us to his characters and help us get to know them and care about what happens to them. And although there may be illustrations, it's still the author's job to carefully choose his words so we see the characters the way he wants us to. He will give you many clues, but you have to pick up on them!*

> *As we read this story, really pay attention to the main characters—what they look like and what kind of people they are. We'll study the clues that help us see the characters a certain way. In other words, if you think something about a character, you'll have to examine what in the story leads you to see him that way. Was it something the character did or said? You're going to need to be active thinkers.*

Show students the graphic organizer.

> *This chart will help you organize and examine your thoughts. After you read, ask yourself what you think about the main character. Write your thoughts on the left side, and on the right, record what happens in the story or what words the author used to make you think this. Then, we'll compare our thoughts. Remember, there will be differences because we all bring our schema— our unique backgrounds and experiences—to everything we read.*

What I think about Mark	Proof from the story:
Mark is a good person.	He tries to teach Kelly things since she can't go to school and he makes sure she has enough food to eat.

After reading: After most students have recorded their character observations, begin sharing and discussing. The goal is for students to be able to pinpoint what words in the story helped them to define the character.

Different Strategies for Different Questions

It's a fact of life that our students will be expected to answer questions about what they have read, either on work sheets or standardized tests. Now that you've taught your students to be adept at tuning into the questions they have while they read, it's time to prepare them to answer questions that others will ask them.

Before reading: This lesson is based on *Alexander and the Terrible, Horrible, No Good, Very Bad Day* by Judith Viorst, but any book can be used. Choose one that you have multiple copies of, however, as students will need to refer to the text to answer questions. Here are questions we've used with this book, but you can make up your own. Make a copy of the questions for each student or write them on the board.

- Why did the dad get mad when the kids came to his office?
- Was it fair that Alexander had to have plain shoes? Explain your answer.
- Who do you think should have been in trouble when the boys got in a fight by the car? Why?
- What did Alexander's brother find in his breakfast cereal?
- Were Alexander's brothers being nice to him? Explain your answer.
- Where did Alexander say he was going to move?
- What could have helped Alexander have a better day?

Before reading the book to students, review with them the kinds of questions that require inference and those that are literal. Next, show students your list of questions and together sort them as to whether the answer would be found, literally, in the text or whether readers would need to infer to figure out the answer. If you write your questions on sentence strips, you can arrange them on the board in two columns, one for literal questions and the other for inferential questions. Now you are ready to read the book to your students.

Sample mini-lesson

" *Remember when we talked about the difference between literal and inferential questions? The answers to literal questions can be found right in the text, and often you can scan to find the answer quickly.*

" *Inferential questions are the kind you have to think about. You have to take the clues the author gives you and add what you already know to figure out the answer.*

Read the story to students.

" *Okay boys and girls, now that you have heard the story, let's look again at the questions we* sorted. Are there any you want to switch to the other column? If you think a question should be switched from the literal column to the inferential one, be ready to explain your reasons to us.

" All right, now that we know what kind of questions they are, we need to answer them. Knowing what kind of question you have is half the battle because you will know what to do to answer it. For the literal questions, we need to look back into the book and find the answers. Use what you have learned about scanning for these. For the inferential questions, we have to find clues from the book, but we also need to think! We have to use what we know and add that to the clues and information from the book to figure out the answer.

" I'll assign partners and give each team a copy of the book. You will work together to answer the questions. For the inferential questions, I want you to record what the information from the text was and what your thoughts were that helped you come up with your answer.

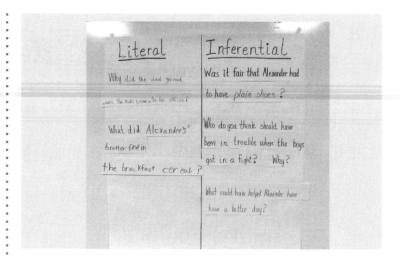

During reading: While partners are reading and working on answering the questions, make notes about which students are having trouble scanning to find the literal answers and which students are having trouble inferring. Then plan groups as needed to provide more practice and support to these students.

After reading: Review with students the importance of thinking about the types of questions they are asked to answer. Discuss the strategies for finding the answers to each kind of question. If it is a literal question, remind them to scan the text for the answer. If it is an inferential question, remind them to look for clues and be ready to think!

Recommended Reading & Reproducibles

Clay, Marie M. *Records for Classroom Teachers*. Portsmouth, NH: Heinemann Publishing, 2000.

Collins, Kathy. *Growing Readers: Units of Study in the Primary Classroom.* Portland, ME: Stenhouse Publishers, 2004.

Harvey, Stephanie, and Anne Goudvis. *Strategies That Work: Teaching Comprehension to Enhance Understanding.* Portland, ME: Stenhouse Publishers, 2000.

Hoyt, Linda. *Spotlight on Comprehension: Building a Literacy of Thoughtfulness.* Portsmouth, NH: Heinemann Publishing, 2004.

Keene, Ellin Oliver, and Susan Zimmermann. *Mosaic of Thought: Teaching Comprehension in a Reader's Workshop.* Portsmouth, NH: Heinemann Publishing, 1997.

Miller, Debbie. *Reading with Meaning: Teaching Comprehension in the Primary Grades.* Portland, ME: Stenhouse Publishers, 2002.

National Reading Panel, www.nationalreadingpanel.org

Rasinski, Timothy V. *The Fluent Reader: Oral Reading Strategies for Building Word Recognition, Fluency, and Comprehension.* New York, NY: Scholastic, 2003.

Routman, Regie. *Reading Essentials: The Specifics You Need to Teach Reading Well.* Portsmouth, NH: Heinemann Publishing, 2002.

Vygotsky, L. S. *Mind in Society: The Development of Higher Psychological Processes.* Cambridge, MA: Harvard University Press, 2006.

Zimmermann, Susan, and Chryse Hutchins. *7 Keys to Comprehension.* New York, NY: Three Rivers Press, 2003.

Decoding Strategies

 Look at the pictures for clues.

 Start the tricky word.

 Think about what would make sense.

 Skip the word and return to fix it.

 Look for chunks you already know within larger words.

 Switch the vowel sound.

Decoding Strategies

 Look at the pictures for clues.

 Start the tricky word.

 Think about what would make sense.

 Skip the word and return to fix it.

 Look for chunks you already know within larger words.

 Switch the vowel sound.

Individual Strategy Use Assessment

Name _____

Date _____

Title _____ Fiction _____ Nonfiction _____ Level _____

Strategy	Uses Strategy		Comments
Look at the picture for clues.	Yes	No	
Start the tricky word.	Yes	No	
Think about what makes sense.	Yes	No	
Skip the word and return to fix it.	Yes	No	
Look for chunks you already know within larger words.	Yes	No	
Switch the vowel sound.	Yes	No	

Class-at-a-Glance Strategy Use Record

Name	Date	Looks at the picture	Starts the tricky word	Thinks about what makes sense	Reads on and returns	Looks for chunks	Switches the vowel sound	Notes:

Get Your Brain Started And Give It Directions!

How?

Read the title and
THINK!

Read the back and
THINK!

Look through the book and
THINK!

*Now your brain is
ready to read!*

Get Your Brain Started And Give It Directions!

How?

Read the title and
THINK!

Read the back and
THINK!

Look through the book and
THINK!

*Now your brain is
ready to read!*

What Did You Think?

What did you think
after reading the **title**?

_____

_____

_____

What did you think
after reading the **back**?

_____

_____

_____

What did you think
after looking **through** the book?

_____

_____

_____

What did you think
after reading the **title**?

_____

_____

_____

What did you think
after reading the **back**?

_____

_____

_____

What did you think
after looking **through** the book?

_____

_____

_____

Use Your Metacognition
Is your brain on the right road?

✔**Check to be sure!**

CAN YOU . . .

Tell the main ideas?

Predict what might happen next?

Do you understand everything?

IF NOT . . .

Reread! Reread! Reread!

Think about what has
happened so far.

Read on and then stop
to think again!

*Know when you know,
and when you don't!*

Use Your Metacognition
Is your brain on the right road?

✔**Check to be sure!**

CAN YOU . . .

Tell the main ideas?

Predict what might happen next?

Do you understand everything?

IF NOT . . .

Reread! Reread! Reread!

Think about what has
happened so far.

Read on and then stop
to think again!

*Know when you know,
and when you don't!*

How's the Movie?
Do you see it?

✔ **Check to be sure!**

ASK YOURSELF:

Do you see it?

Does it make sense?

IF NOT . . .

Reread! Reread! Reread!

Go back and think!

If you can see the movie,
I hope you enjoy the
rest of the book!

*Know when you know,
and when you don't!*

How's the Movie?
Do you see it?

✔ **Check to be sure!**

ASK YOURSELF:

Do you see it?

Does it make sense?

IF NOT . . .

Reread! Reread! Reread!

Go back and think!

If you can see the movie,
I hope you enjoy the
rest of the book!

*Know when you know,
and when you don't!*

Turn and Talk

1. Make eye contact.
2. Be respectful.
3. Stay on task.

Punctuation

When we see _____, our voice _____.

. = **Drops and stops**

! = **Gets excited and stops**

? = **Goes up and stops**

, = **Takes a short rest**

" " = **Gets to be an actor**

_____'s Reading Rate Record

Words Per Minute	Date	Date	Date	Date	Date	Date	Date	Date
120+								
110-119								
100-109								
90-99								
80-89								
70-79								
60-69								
50-59								
40-49								
30-39								
20-29								
10-19								
0-9								
Notes								

Fluency Rubric

Reader _____ Partner _____

	1st Reading	2nd Reading	3rd Reading
Expression and punctuation	1 2 3	1 2 3	1 2 3
Phrasing Word by word 1 Some phrasing 2 Good phrasing 3	1 2 3	1 2 3	1 2 3

- -

Fluency Rubric

Reader _____ Partner _____

	1st Reading	2nd Reading	3rd Reading
Expression and punctuation	1 2 3	1 2 3	1 2 3
Phrasing Word by word 1 Some phrasing 2 Good phrasing 3	1 2 3	1 2 3	1 2 3

Name _____

Main Idea and Details

Main Idea: _____

Detail:

Detail:

Detail:

Nonfiction
Set a Purpose for Reading

Name _____

Record the heading and predict what you think you will learn about. Write one question the heading makes you wonder about. Read the section and then write what the section was about.

Heading _____

Prediction _____

Question _____

What was it about? _____

_____

_____

Heading _____

Prediction _____

Question _____

What was it about? _____

_____

_____

My Connections

Name _____

Text:	My connection	How my connection helps me understand
Pg.#		

Many Connections

Name _____

Text-to-Self	Text-to-Text	Text-to-World

Connect to Understand

Name _____

My Connection	Pg.#	What It Helps Me Understand

Do You See What I See?

Name _____

I see . . .	Now I see . . .

My Visualization

Name _____

My visualization . . .	The text says. . .
Stopping page _____	
Stopping page _____	
Stopping page _____	

Do the Math—Make the Inferences

Name _____

Clues from the text:	+	What I know:

My inference:

Clues from the text:	+	What I know:

My inference:

What Does It Mean?

Name _____

Word _____

What I think it means: _____

_____

What in the text makes me think I'm right: _____

_____

_____

Word _____

What I think it means: _____

_____

What in the text makes me think I'm right: _____

_____

_____

Word _____

What I think it means: _____

_____

What in the text makes me think I'm right: _____

_____

_____

What I Think About

Name _____

What I think about _____ Proof from the story: